SECOND VATICAN COUNCIL

PASTORAL CONSTITUTION ON THE CHURCH IN THE MODERN WORLD

Gaudium et Spes

December 7, 1965

*Discussion Outline and Bibliography by
Reverend Donald R. Campion, SJ, Ph.D.,
sociologist and former associate editor of
AMERICA. Father Campion was in atten-
dance at the 1963, 1964, and 1965 sessions
of Vatican Council II.*

Publication No. 015-X
United States Catholic Conference
Washington, D.C.
ISBN 1-55586-015-X

Published in the United States, Ninth Printing, February 1996

PAUL, BISHOP, SERVANT OF THE SERVANTS OF GOD TOGETHER WITH THE FATHERS OF THE SACRED COUNCIL

FOR EVERLASTING MEMORY

PASTORAL CONSTITUTION[1] ON THE CHURCH IN THE MODERN WORLD

PREFACE

1. The joys and the hopes, the griefs and the anxieties of the men of this age, especially those who are poor or in any way afflicted, these are the joys and hopes, the griefs and anxieties of the followers of Christ. Indeed, nothing genuinely human fails to raise an echo in their hearts. For theirs is a community composed of men. United in Christ, they are led by the Holy Spirit in their journey to the Kingdom of their Father and they have welcomed the news of salvation which is meant for every man. That is why this community realizes that it is truly linked with mankind and its history by the deepest of bonds.

2.   Hence this Second Vatican Council, having probed more profoundly into the mystery of the Church, now addresses itself without hesitation, not only to the sons of the Church and to all who invoke the name of Christ, but to the whole of humanity. For the Council yearns to explain to everyone how it conceives of the presence and activity of the Church in the world of today.

Therefore, the Council focuses its attention on the world of men, the whole human family along with the sum of those realities in the midst of which it lives; that world which is the theater of man's history, and the heir of his energies, his tragedies and his triumphs; that world which the Christian sees as created and sustained by its Maker's love, fallen indeed into the bondage of sin, yet emancipated now by Christ, Who was crucified and rose again to break the stranglehold of personified evil, so that the world might be fashioned anew according to God's design and reach its fulfillment.

3.   Though mankind is stricken with wonder at its own discoveries and its power, it often raises anxious questions about the current trend of the world, about the place and role of man in the universe, about the meaning of its individual and collective strivings, and about the ultimate destiny of reality and of humanity. Hence, giving witness and voice to the faith of the whole People of God gathered together by Christ, this Council can provide no more eloquent proof of its solidarity with, as well as its respect and love for the entire human family with which it is bound up, than by engaging with it in conversation about these various problems. The Council brings to mankind light kindled from the Gospel, and puts at its disposal those saving resources which the Church herself, under the guidance of the Holy Spirit, receives from her Founder. For the human person deserves to be preserved; human society deserves to be renewed. Hence the focal point of our total presentation will be man himself, whole and entire, body and soul, heart and conscience, mind and will.

Therefore, this Sacred Synod, proclaiming the noble destiny of man and championing the godlike seed which has been sown in him, offers to mankind the honest assistance of the Church in fostering that brotherhood of all men which corresponds to this destiny of theirs. Inspired by no earthly ambition, the Church seeks but a solitary goal: to carry forward the work of Christ under the lead of the befriending Spirit. And Christ entered this world to give witness to the truth, to rescue and not to sit in judgment, to serve and not to be served.[2]

INTRODUCTORY STATEMENT

The Situation of Men in the Modern World

4.   T o carry out such a task, the Church has always had the duty of scrutinizing the signs of the times and of interpreting them in the light of the Gospel. Thus, in language intelligible to each generation, she can respond to the perennial questions which men ask about this present life and the life to come, and about the relationship of the one to the other. We must therefore recognize and understand the world in which we live, its expectations, its longings, and its often dramatic characteristics. Some of the main features of the modern world can be sketched as follows.

Today, the human race is involved in a new stage of history. Profound and rapid changes are spreading by degrees around the whole world. Triggered by the intelligence and creative energies of man, these changes recoil upon him, upon his decisions and desires, both individual and collective, and upon his manner of thinking and acting with respect to things and to people. Hence we can already speak of a true cultural and social transformation, one which has repercussions on man's religious life as well.

As happens in any crisis of growth, this transformation has brought serious difficulties in its wake. Thus while man extends his power in every direction, he does not always succeed in subjecting it to his own welfare. Striving to probe more profoundly into the deeper recesses of his own mind, he frequently appears more unsure of himself. Gradually and more precisely he lays bare the laws of society, only to be paralyzed by uncertainty about the direction to give it.

Never has the human race enjoyed such an abundance of wealth, resources and economic power, and yet a huge proportion of the world's citizens are still tormented by hunger and poverty, while countless numbers suffer from total illiteracy. Never before has man had so keen an understanding of freedom, yet at the same time, new forms of social and psychological slavery make their appearance. Although the world of today has a very vivid awareness of its unity and of how one man depends on another in needful solidarity, it is most grievously torn into opposing camps by conflicting forces. For political, social, economic, racial and ideological disputes still continue bitterly, and with them the peril of a war which would reduce everything to ashes. True, there is a growing exchange of ideas, but the very words by which key concepts are expressed take on quite different meanings in diverse ideological systems. Finally, man painstakingly searches for a better world, without a corresponding spiritual advancement.

Influenced by such a variety of complexities, many of our contemporaries are kept from accurately identifying permanent values and adjusting them properly to fresh discoveries. As a result, buffeted between hope and anxiety and pressing one another with questions about the present course of events, they are burdened down with uneasiness. This same course of events leads men to look for answers; indeed, it forces them to do so.

5. Today's spiritual agitation and the changing conditions of life are part of a broader and deeper revolution. As a result of the latter, intellectual formation is ever increasingly based on the mathematical and natural sciences and on those dealing with man himself, while in the practical order the technology which stems from these sciences takes on mounting importance.

This scientific spirit has a new kind of impact on the cultural sphere and on modes of thought. Technology is now transforming the face of the earth, and is already trying to master outer space. To a certain extent, the human intellect is also broadening its dominion over time: over the past by means of historical knowledge; over the future, by the art of projecting and by planning.

5

Advances in biology, psychology, and the social sciences not only bring men hope of improved self-knowledge; in conjunction with technical methods, they are helping men exert direct influence on the life of social groups.

At the same time, the human race is giving steadily increasing thought to forecasting and regulating its own population growth. History itself speeds along on so rapid a course that an individual person can scarcely keep abreast of it. The destiny of the human community has become all of a piece, where once the various groups of men had a kind of private history of their own.

Thus, the human race has passed from a rather static concept of reality to a more dynamic, evolutionary one. In consequence there has arisen a new series of problems, a series as numerous as can be, calling for new efforts of analysis and synthesis.

6. By this very circumstance, the traditional local communities such as families, clans, tribes, villages, various groups and associations stemming from social contacts, experience more thorough changes every day.

The industrial type of society is gradually being spread, leading some nations to economic affluence, and radically transforming ideas and social conditions established for centuries.

Likewise, the cult and pursuit of city living has grown, either because of a multiplication of cities and their inhabitants, or by a transplantation of city life to rural settings.

New and more efficient media of social communication are contributing to the knowledge of events; by setting off chain reactions they are giving the swiftest and widest possible circulation to styles of thought and feeling.

It is also noteworthy how many men are being induced to migrate on various counts, and are thereby changing their manner of life. Thus a man's ties with his fellows are constantly being multiplied, and at the same time "socialization" brings further ties, without, however, always promoting appropriate personal development and truly personal relationships.

This kind of evolution can be seen more clearly in those nations which already enjoy the conveniences of economic and technological progress, though it is also astir among peoples still striving for such progress and eager to secure for themselves the advantages of an industrialized and urbanized society. These peoples, especially those among them who are attached to older traditions, are simultaneously undergoing a movement toward more mature and personal exercise of liberty.

7. A change in attitudes and in human structures frequently calls accepted values into question, especially among young people, who have grown impatient on more than one occasion, and indeed become rebels in their distress. Aware of their own influence in the life of society, they want a part in it sooner. This frequently causes parents and educators to experience greater difficulties day by day in discharging their tasks. The institutions, laws and modes of thinking and feeling as handed down from previous generations do not always seem to be well adapted to the contemporary state of affairs; hence arises an upheaval in the manner and even the norms of behavior.

Finally, these new conditions have their impact on religion. On the one hand, a more critical ability to distinguish religion from a magical view of the world and from the superstitions which still circulate purifies it and exacts day by day a more personal and explicit adherence to faith. As a result many persons are achieving a more vivid sense of God. On the other hand, growing numbers of people are abandoning religion in practice. Unlike former days, the denial of God or of religion, or the abandonment of them, are no longer unusual and individual occurrences. For today it is not rare for such things to be presented as requirements of scientific progress or of a certain new humanism. In numerous places these views are voiced not only in the teachings of philosophers, but on every side they influence literature, the arts, the interpretation of the humanities and of history and civil laws themselves. As a consequence, many people are shaken.

8. This development coming so rapidly and often in a disorderly fashion, combined with keener awareness itself of the

inequalities in the world beget or intensify contradictions and imbalances.

Within the individual person there develops rather frequently an imbalance between an intellect which is modern in practical matters, and a theoretical system of thought which can neither master the sum total of its ideas, nor arrange them adequately into a synthesis. Likewise an imbalance arises between a concern for practicality and efficiency, and the demands of moral conscience; also very often between the conditions of collective existence and the requisites of personal thought, and even of contemplation. At length there develops an imbalance between specialized human activity and a comprehensive view of reality.

As for the family, discord results from population, economic and social pressures, or from difficulties which arise between succeeding generations, or from new social relationships between men and women.

Differences crop up too between races and between various kinds of social orders; between wealthy nations and those which are less influential or are needy; finally, between international institutions born of the popular desire for peace, and the ambition to propagate one's own ideology, as well as collective greed existing in nations or other groups.

What results is mutual distrust, enmities, conflicts and hardships. Of such is man at once the cause and the victim.

9. Meanwhile the conviction grows not only that humanity can and should increasingly consolidate its control over creation, but even more, that it devolves on humanity to establish a political, social and economic order which will increasingly serve man and help individuals as well as groups to affirm and develop the dignity proper to them.

As a result many persons are quite aggressively demanding those benefits of which with vivid awareness they judge themselves to be deprived either through injustice or unequal distribution. Nations on the road to progress, like those recently made independent, desire to participate in the goods of modern civilization, not only in the political field but also economically, and to play their part freely on the world scene. Still they continually fall behind while very often their economic and other forms of dependence on wealthier nations increases more rapidly.

People hounded by hunger call upon those better off. Where they have not yet won it, women claim for themselves an equity with men before the law and in fact. Laborers and farmers seek not only to provide for the necessities of life, but to develop the gifts of their personality by their labors and indeed to take part in regulating economic, social, political and cultural life. Now, for the first time in human history all people are convinced that the benefits of culture ought to be and actually can be extended to everyone.

Still, beneath all these demands lies a deeper and more widespread longing: persons and societies thirst for a full and free life worthy of man; one in which they can subject to their own welfare all that the modern world can offer them so abundantly. In addition, nations try harder every day to bring about a kind of universal community.

Since all these things are so, the modern world shows itself at once powerful and weak, capable of the noblest deeds or the foulest; before it lies the path to freedom or to slavery, to progress or retreat, to brotherhood or hatred. Moreover, man is becoming aware that it is his responsibility to guide aright the forces which he has unleashed and which can enslave him or minister to him. That is why he is putting questions to himself.

10.   The truth is that the imbalances under which the modern world labors are linked with that more basic imbalance which is rooted in the heart of man. For in man himself many elements wrestle with one another. Thus, on the one hand, as a creature he experiences his limitations in a multitude of ways; on the other he feels himself to be boundless in his desires and summoned to a higher life. Pulled by manifold attractions he is constantly forced to choose among them and to renounce some. Indeed, as a weak and sinful being, he often does what he would not, and fails to do

what he would.[1] Hence he suffers from internal divisions, and from these flow so many and such great discords in society. No doubt many whose lives are infected with a practical materialism are blinded against any sharp insight into this kind of dramatic situation; or else, weighed down by unhappiness they are prevented from giving the matter any thought. Thinking they have found serenity in an interpretation of reality everywhere proposed these days, many look forward to a genuine and total emancipation of humanity wrought solely by human effort; they are convinced that the future rule of man over the earth will satisfy every desire of his heart. Nor are there lacking men who despair of any meaning to life and praise the boldness of those who think that human existence is devoid of any inherent significance and strive to confer a total meaning on it by their own ingenuity alone.

Nevertheless, in the face of the modern development of the world, the number constantly swells of the people who raise the most basic questions or recognize them with a new sharpness: what is man? What is this sense of sorrow, of evil, of death, which continues to exist despite so much progress? What purpose have these victories secured at so high a cost? What can man offer to society, what can he expect from it? What follows this earthly life?

The Church firmly believes that Christ, who died and was raised up for all,[2] can through His Spirit offer man the light and the strength to measure up to his supreme destiny. Nor has any other name under heaven been given to man by which it is fitting for him to be saved.[3] She likewise holds that in her most benign Lord and Master can be found the key, the focal point and the goal of man, as well as of all human history. The Church also maintains that beneath all changes there are many realities which do not change and which have their ultimate foundation in Christ, Who is the same yesterday and today, yes and forever.[4] Hence under the light of Christ, the image of the unseen God, the firstborn of every creature,[5] the Council wishes to speak to all men in order to shed light on the mystery of man and to cooperate in finding the solution to the outstanding problems of our time.

PART I

THE CHURCH
AND MAN'S CALLING

11. The People of God believes that it is led by the Lord's Spirit, Who fills the earth. Motivated by this faith, it labors to decipher authentic signs of God's presence and purpose in the happenings, needs and desires in which this People has a part along with other men of our age. For faith throws a new light on everything, manifests God's design for man's total vocation, and thus directs the mind to solutions which are fully human.

This Council, first of all, wishes to assess in this light those values which are most highly prized today and to relate them to their divine source. Insofar as they stem from endowments conferred by God on man, these values are exceedingly good. Yet they are often wrenched from their rightful function by the taint in man's heart, and hence stand in need of purification.

What does the Church think of man? What needs to be recommended for the upbuilding of contemporary society? What is the ultimate significance of human activity throughout the world? People are waiting for an answer to these questions. From the answers it will be increasingly clear that the People of God and the human race in whose midst it lives render service to each other. Thus the mission of the Church will show its religious, and by that very fact, its supremely human character.

CHAPTER I

THE DIGNITY OF
THE HUMAN PERSON

12.   According to the almost unanimous opinion of believers and unbelievers alike, all things on earth should be related to man as their center and crown.

But what is man? About himself he has expressed, and continues to express, many divergent and even contradictory opinions. In these he often exalts himself as the absolute measure of all things or debases himself to the point of despair. The result is doubt and anxiety. The Church certainly understands these problems. Endowed with light from God, she can offer solutions to them, so that man's true situation can be portrayed and his defects explained, while at the same time his dignity and destiny are justly acknowledged.

For Sacred Scripture teaches that man was created "to the image of God," is capable of knowing and loving his Creator, and was appointed by Him as master of all earthly creatures[1] that he might subdue them and use them to God's glory.[2] "What is man that you should care for him? You have made him little less than the angels, and crowned him with glory and honor. You have given him rule over the works of your hands, putting all things under his feet." (Ps. 8:5-7).

But God did not create man to be alone, for from the beginning "male and female he created them" (Gen. 1:27). Their companionship produces the primary form of interpersonal communion. For by his innermost nature man is a social being, and unless he relates himself to others he can neither live nor develop his potential.

Therefore, as we read elsewhere in Holy Scripture, God saw "all that he had made, and it was very good" (Gen. 1:31).

13. Although he was made by God in a state of holiness, from the very beginning of his history man abused his liberty, at the urging of the Evil One. Man set himself against God and sought to attain his goal apart from God. Although they knew God, they did not glorify Him as God, but their senseless minds were darkened and they served the creature rather than the Creator.[3] What divine revelation makes known to us conforms with experience. Examining his heart, man finds that he has inclinations toward evil too, and is engulfed by manifold ills which cannot come from his good Creator. Often refusing to acknowledge God as his beginning, man has disrupted also his proper relationship to his own ultimate goal as well as his whole relationship toward himself and others and all created things.

Therefore man is split within himself. As a result, all of human life, whether individual or collective, shows itself to be a dramatic struggle between good and evil, between light and darkness. Indeed, man finds that by himself he is incapable of battling the assaults of evil successfully, so that everyone feels as though he is bound by chains. But the Lord Himself came to free and strengthen man, renewing him inwardly and casting out that "prince of this world" (John 12:31) who held him in the bondage of sin.[4] For sin has diminished man, blocking his path to fulfillment.

The call to grandeur and the depths of misery, both of which are a part of human experience, find their ultimate and simultaneous explanation in the light of this revelation.

14. Though made of body and soul, man is one. Through his bodily composition he gathers to himself the elements of the material world; thus they reach their crown through him, and through him raise their voice in free praise of the Creator.[5] For this reason man is not allowed to despise his bodily life; rather he is obliged to regard his body as good and honorable since God has created it and will raise it up on the last day. Nevertheless wounded by sin, man experiences rebellious stirrings in his body. But the

13

very dignity of man postulates that man glorify God in his body[6] and forbids it to serve the evil inclinations of his heart.

Now, man is not wrong when he regards himself as superior to bodily concerns, and as more than a speck of nature or a nameless constituent of the city of man. For by his interior qualities he outstrips the whole sum of mere things. He plunges into the depths of reality whenever he enters into his own heart; God, Who probes the heart,[7] awaits him there; there he discerns his proper destiny beneath the eyes of God. Thus, when he recognizes in himself a spiritual and immortal soul, he is not being mocked by a fantasy born only of physical or social influences, but is rather laying hold of the proper truth of the matter.

15.   Man judges rightly that by his intellect he surpasses the material universe, for he shares in the light of the divine mind. By relentlessly employing his talents through the ages he has indeed made progress in the practical sciences and in technology and the liberal arts. In our times he has won superlative victories, especially in his probing of the material world and in subjecting it to himself. Still he has always searched for more penetrating truths, and finds them. For his intelligence is not confined to observable data alone, but can with genuine certitude attain to reality itself as knowable, though in consequence of sin that certitude is partly obscured and weakened.

The intellectual nature of the human person is perfected by wisdom and needs to be, for wisdom gently attracts the mind of man to a quest and a love for what is true and good. Steeped in wisdom, man passes through visible realities to those which are unseen.

Our era needs such wisdom more than bygone ages if the discoveries made by man are to be further humanized. For the future of the world stands in peril unless wiser men are forthcoming. It should also be pointed out that many nations, poorer in economic goods, are quite rich in wisdom and can offer noteworthy advantages to others.

It is, finally, through the gift of the Holy Spirit that man comes by faith to the contemplation and appreciation of the divine plan.[8]

16. In the depths of his conscience, man detects a law which he does not impose upon himself, but which holds him to obedience. Always summoning him to love good and avoid evil, the voice of conscience when necessary speaks to his heart: do this, shun that. For man has in his heart a law written by God; to obey it is the very dignity of man; according to it he will be judged.[9] Conscience is the most secret core and sanctuary of a man. There he is alone with God, Whose voice echoes in his depths.[10] In a wonderful manner conscience reveals that law which is fulfilled by love of God and neighbor.[11] In fidelity to conscience, Christians are joined with the rest of men in the search for truth, and for the genuine solution to the numerous problems which arise in the life of individuals and from social relationships. Hence the more correct conscience holds sway, the more persons and groups turn aside from blind choice and strive to be guided by the objective norms of morality. Conscience frequently errs from invincible ignorance without losing its dignity. The same cannot be said for a man who cares but little for truth and goodness, or for a conscience which by degrees grows practically sightless as a result of habitual sin.

17. Only in freedom can man direct himself toward goodness. Our contemporaries make much of this freedom and pursue it eagerly; and rightly to be sure. Often, however, they foster it perversely as a license for doing whatever pleases them, even if it is evil. For its part, authentic freedom is an exceptional sign of the divine image within man. For God has willed that man remain "under the control of his own decisions,"[12] so that he can seek his Creator spontaneously, and come freely to utter and blissful perfection through loyalty to Him. Hence man's dignity demands that he act according to a knowing and free choice that is personally motivated and prompted from within, not under blind internal impulse nor by mere external pressure. Man achieves such dignity when, emancipating himself from all captivity to passion, he pursues his goal in a spontaneous choice of what is good and procures for himself, through effective and skilful action, aids to that end.

15

Since man's freedom has been damaged by sin, only by the aid of God's grace can he bring such a relationship with God into full flower. Before the judgment seat of God each man must render an account of his own life, whether he has done good or evil.[13]

18. It is in the face of death that the riddle of human existence grows most acute. Not only is man tormented by pain and by the advancing deterioration of his body, but even more so by a dread of perpetual extinction. He rightly follows the intuition of his heart when he abhors and repudiates the utter ruin and total disappearance of his own person. He rebels against death because he bears in himself an eternal seed which cannot be reduced to sheer matter. All the endeavors of technology, though useful in the extreme, cannot calm his anxiety; for a prolongation of biological life is unable to satisfy that desire for a higher life which is inescapably lodged in his breast.

Although the mystery of death utterly beggars the imagination, the Church has been taught by divine revelation and firmly teaches that man has been created by God for a blissful purpose beyond the reach of earthly misery. In addition, that bodily death from which man would have been immune had he not sinned[14] will be vanquished, according to the Christian faith, when man who was ruined by his own doing is restored to wholeness by an almighty and merciful Saviour. For God has called man and still calls him so that with his entire being he might be joined to Him in an endless sharing of a divine life beyond all corruption. Christ won this victory when He rose to life, for by His death He freed man from death.[15] Hence to every thoughtful man a solidly established faith provides the answer to his anxiety about what the future holds for him. At the same time faith gives him the power to be united in Christ with his loved ones who have already been snatched away by death; faith arouses the hope that they have found true life with God.

19. The basic source of human dignity lies in man's call to communion with God. From the very circumstance of his origin man is already invited to converse with God. For man would not exist were he not created by God's love and constantly preserved

16

by it; and he cannot live fully according to truth unless he freely acknowledges that love and devotes himself to His Creator. Still, many of our contemporaries have never recognized this intimate and vital link with God, or have explicitly rejected it. Thus atheism must be accounted among the most serious problems of this age, and is deserving of closer examination.

The word atheism is applied to phenomena which are quite distinct from one another. For while God is expressly denied by some, others believe that man can assert absolutely nothing about Him. Still others use such a method to scrutinize the question of God as to make it seem devoid of meaning. Many, unduly transgressing the limits of the positive sciences, contend that everything can be explained by this kind of scientific reasoning alone or, by contrast, they altogether disallow the fact that there is any absolute truth. Some laud man so extravagantly that their faith in God lapses into a kind of anemia, though they seem more inclined to affirm man than to deny God. Again some form for themselves such a fallacious idea of God that when they repudiate this figment they are by no means rejecting the God of the Gospel. Some never get to the point of raising questions about God, since they seem to experience no religious stirrings nor do they see why they should trouble themselves about religion. Moreover, atheism results not rarely from a violent protest against the evil in this world, or from the absolute character with which certain human values are unduly invested, and which thereby already accords them the stature of God. Modern civilization itself often complicates the approach to God not for any essential reason but because it is so heavily engrossed in earthly affairs.

Undeniably, those who willfully shut out God from their hearts and try to dodge religious questions are not following the dictates of their consciences, and hence are not free of blame; yet believers themselves frequently bear some responsibility for this situation. For, taken as a whole, atheism is not a spontaneous development but stems from a variety of causes, including a critical reaction against religious beliefs, and in some places against the Christian religion in particular. Hence believers can have more than a little to do with

17

the birth of atheism. To the extent that they neglect their own training in the faith, or teach erroneous doctrine, or are deficient in their religious, moral or social life, they must be said to conceal rather than reveal the authentic face of God and religion.

20. Modern atheism often takes on a systematic expression which, in addition to other causes, stretches the desire for human independence to such a point that it poses difficulties against any kind of dependence on God. Those who profess atheism of this sort maintain that it gives man freedom to be an end unto himself, the sole artisan and creator of his own history. They claim that this freedom cannot be reconciled with the affirmation of a Lord Who is author and purpose of all things, or at least that this freedom makes such an affirmation altogether superfluous. The sense of power which modern technical progress generates in man can nourish this belief.

Not to be overlooked among the forms of modern atheism is that which anticipates the liberation of man especially through his economic and social emancipation. This form argues that by its nature religion thwarts this liberation by arousing man's hope for a deceptive future life, thereby diverting him from the constructing of the earthly city. Consequently when the proponents of this doctrine gain governmental power they vigorously fight against religion, and promote atheism by using, especially in the education of youth, those means of pressure which public power has at its disposal.

21. In her loyal devotion to God and men, the Church has already repudiated[16] and cannot cease repudiating, sorrowfully but as firmly as possible, those poisonous doctrines and actions which contradict reason and the common experience of humanity, and dethrone man from his native excellence.

Still, she strives to detect in the atheistic mind the hidden causes for the denial of God; conscious of how weighty are the questions which atheism raises, and motivated by love for all men, she believes these questions ought to be examined seriously and more profoundly.

18

The Church holds that the recognition of God is in no way hostile to man's dignity, since this dignity is rooted and perfected in God. For man was made an intelligent and free member of society by the God Who created him; but even more important, he is called as a son to commune with God and share in His happiness. She further teaches that a hope related to the end of time does not diminish the importance of intervening duties but rather undergirds the acquittal of them with fresh incentives. By contrast, when a divine substructure and the hope of life eternal are wanting, man's dignity is most grievously lacerated, as current events often attest; the riddles of life and death, of guilt and of grief go unsolved, with the frequent result that men succumb to despair.

Meanwhile every man remains to himself an unsolved puzzle, however obscurely he may perceive it. For on certain occasions no one can entirely escape the kind of self-questioning mentioned earlier, especially when life's major events take place. To this questioning only God fully and most certainly provides an answer as he summons man to higher knowledge and humbler probing.

The remedy which must be applied to atheism, however, is to be sought in a proper presentation of the Church's teaching as well as in the integral life of the Church and her members. For it is the function of the Church, led by the Holy Spirit Who renews and purifies her ceaselessly,[17] to make God the Father and His Incarnate Son present and in a sense visible. This result is achieved chiefly by the witness of a living and mature faith, namely, one trained to see difficulties clearly and to master them. Many martyrs have given luminous witness to this faith and continue to do so. This faith needs to prove its fruitfulness by penetrating the believer's entire life, including its worldly dimensions, and by activating him toward justice and love, especially regarding the needy. What does the most reveal God's presence, however, is the brotherly charity of the faithful who are united in spirit as they work together for the faith of the Gospel[18] and who prove themselves a sign of unity.

While rejecting atheism, root and branch, the Church sincerely professes that all men, believers and unbelievers alike, ought to work for the rightful betterment of this world in which all alike live; such an ideal cannot be realized, however, apart from sincere and prudent dialogue. Hence the Church protests against the distinction which some state authorities make between believers and unbelievers, with prejudice to the fundamental rights of the human person. The Church calls for the active freedom of believers to build up in this world God's temple too. She courteously invites atheists to examine the Gospel of Christ with an open mind.

Above all the Church knows that her message is in harmony with the most secret desires of the human heart when she champions the dignity of the human vocation, restoring hope to those who have already despaired of anything higher than their present lot. Far from diminishing man, her message brings to his development light, life and freedom. Apart from this message nothing will avail to fill up the heart of man: "Thou hast made us for Thyself," O Lord, "and our hearts are restless till they rest in Thee."[19]

22.   The truth is that only in the mystery of the Incarnate Word does the mystery of man take on light. For Adam, the first man, was a figure of Him Who was to come,[20] namely Christ the Lord. Christ, the final Adam, by the revelation of the mystery of the Father and His love, fully reveals man to man himself and makes his supreme calling clear. It is not surprising, then, that in Him all the aforementioned truths find their root and attain their crown.

He Who is "the image of the invisible God" (Col. 1:15),[21] is Himself the perfect man. To the sons of Adam He restores the divine likeness which had been disfigured from the first sin onward. Since human nature as He assumed it was not annulled,[22] by that very fact it has been raised up to a divine dignity in our respect too. For by His incarnation the Son of God has united Himself in some fashion with every man. He worked with human hands, He thought with a human mind, acted by human choice[23] and loved with a human heart. Born of the Virgin Mary, He has truly been made one of us, like us in all things except sin.[24]

20

As an innocent lamb He merited for us life by the free shedding of His own blood. In Him God reconciled us[25] to Himself and among ourselves; from bondage to the devil and sin He delivered us, so that each one of us can say with the Apostle: The Son of God "loved me and gave Himself up for me" (Gal. 2:20). By suffering for us He not only provided us with an example for our imitation,[26] He blazed a trail, and if we follow it, life and death are made holy and take on a new meaning.

The Christian man, conformed to the likeness of that Son Who is the firstborn of many brothers,[27] received "the first-fruits of the Spirit" (Rom. 8:23) by which he becomes capable of discharging the new law of love.[28] Through this Spirit, who is "the pledge of our inheritance" (Eph. 1:14), the whole man is renewed from within, even to the achievement of "the redemption of the body" (Rom. 8:23): "If the Spirit of him who raised Jesus from the dead dwells in you, then he who raised Jesus Christ from the dead will also bring to life your mortal bodies because of his Spirit who dwells in you" (Rom. 8:11).[29] Pressing upon the Christian to be sure, are the need and the duty to battle against evil through manifold tribulations and even to suffer death. But, linked with the paschal mystery and patterned after the dying Christ, he will hasten forward to resurrection in the strength which comes from hope.[30]

All this holds true not only for Christians, but for all men of good will in whose hearts grace works in an unseen way.[31] For, since Christ died for all men,[32] and since the ultimate vocation of man is in fact one, and divine, we ought to believe that the Holy Spirit in a manner known only to God offers to every man the possibility of being associated with this paschal mystery.

Such is the mystery of man, and it is a great one, as seen by believers in the light of Christian revelation. Through Christ and in Christ, the riddles of sorrow and death grow meaningful. Apart from His Gospel, they overwhelm us. Christ has risen, destroying death by His death; He has lavished life upon us[33] so that, as sons in the Son, we can cry out in the Spirit: Abba, Father![34]

21

CHAPTER II

THE COMMUNITY
OF MANKIND

23. One of the salient features of the modern world is the growing interdependence of men one on the other, a development promoted chiefly by modern technical advances. Nevertheless brotherly dialogue among men does not reach its perfection on the level of technical progress, but on the deeper level of interpersonal relationships. These demand a mutual respect for the full spiritual dignity of the person. Christian revelation contributes greatly to the promotion of this communion between persons, and at the same time leads us to a deeper understanding of the laws of social life which the Creator has written into man's moral and spiritual nature.

Since rather recent documents of the Church's teaching authority have dealt at considerable length with Christian doctrine about human society,[1] this Council is merely going to call to mind some of the more basic truths, treating their foundations under the light of revelation. Then it will dwell more at length on certain of their implications having special significance for our day.

24. God, Who has fatherly concern for everyone, has willed that all men should constitute one family and treat one another in a spirit of brotherhood. For having been created in the image of God, Who "from one man has created the whole human race and made them live all over the face of the earth" (Acts 17:26), all men are called to one and the same goal, namely God Himself.

For this reason, love for God and neighbor is the first and greatest commandment. Sacred Scripture, however, teaches us that

22

the love of God cannot be separated from love of neighbor: "If there is any other commandment, it is summed up in this saying: Thou shalt love thy neighbor as thyself . . . Love therefore is the fulfillment of the Law " (Rom. 13:9, 10; cf. I John 4:20). To men growing daily more dependent on one another, and to a world becoming more unified every day, this truth proves to be of paramount importance.

Indeed, the Lord Jesus, when He prayed to the Father, "that all may be one . . . as we are one" (John 17:21, 22) opened up vistas closed to human reason, for He implied a certain likeness between the union of the divine Persons, and the unity of God's sons in truth and charity. This likeness reveals that man, who is the only creature on earth which God willed for itself, cannot fully find himself except through a sincere gift of himself.[2]

25.   Man's social nature makes it evident that the progress of the human person and the advance of society itself hinge on one another. For the beginning, the subject and the goal of all social institutions is and must be the human person, which for its part and by its very nature stands completely in need of social life.[3] Since this social life is not something added on to man, through his dealings with others, through reciprocal duties, and through fraternal dialogue he develops all his gifts and is able to rise to his destiny.

Among those social ties which man needs for his development some, like the family and political community, relate with greater immediacy to his innermost nature; others originate rather from his free decision. In our era, for various reasons, reciprocal ties and mutual dependencies increase day by day and give rise to a variety of associations and organizations, both public and private. This development, which is called socialization, while certainly not without its dangers, brings with it many advantages with respect to consolidating and increasing the qualities of the human person, and safeguarding his rights.[4]

But if by this social life the human person is greatly aided in responding to his destiny, even in its religious dimensions, it cannot be denied that men are often diverted from doing good and spurred toward evil by the social circumstances in which they live and are immersed from their birth. To be sure the disturbances which so frequently occur in the social order result in part from the natural tensions of economic, political and social forms. But at a deeper level they flow from man's pride and selfishness, which contaminate even the social sphere. When the structure of affairs is flawed by the consequences of sin, man, already born with a bent toward evil, finds there new inducements to sin, which cannot be overcome without strenuous efforts and the assistance of grace.

26. Every day human interdependence tightens and spreads by degrees over the whole world. As a result the common good, that is, the sum of those conditions of social life which allow social groups and their individual members relatively thorough and ready access to their own fulfillment, today takes on an increasingly universal complexion and consequently involves rights and duties with respect to the whole human race. Every social group must take account of the needs and legitimate aspirations of other groups, and even of the general welfare of the entire human family.[5]

At the same time, however, there is a growing awareness of the exalted dignity proper to the human person, since he stands above all things, and his rights and duties are universal and inviolable. Therefore, there must be made available to all men everything necessary for leading a life truly human, such as food, clothing, and shelter; the right to choose a state of life freely and to found a family, the right to education, to employment, to a good reputation, to respect, to appropriate information, to activity in accord with the upright norm of one's own conscience, to protection of privacy and to rightful freedom, even in matters religious.

Hence, the social order and its development must always work to the benefit of the human person if the disposition of affairs is to be subordinate to the personal realm and not contrariwise, as the Lord indicated when He said that the Sabbath was made for man, and not man for the Sabbath.[6]

This social order requires constant improvement. It must be founded on truth, built on justice and animated by love; in freedom it should grow every day toward a more humane balance.[7] An improvement in attitudes and numerous changes in society will have to take place if these objectives are to be gained.

God's Spirit, Who with a marvelous providence directs the unfolding of time and renews the face of the earth, is not absent from this development. The ferment of the Gospel too has aroused and continues to arouse in man's heart the irresistible requirements of his dignity.

27. Coming down to practical and particularly urgent consequences, this Council lays stress on reverence for man; everyone must consider his every neighbor without exception as another self, taking into account first of all his life and the means necessary to living it with dignity,[8] so as not to imitate the rich man who had no concern for the poor man Lazarus.[9]

In our times a special obligation binds us to make ourselves the neighbor of every person without exception, and of actively helping him when he comes across our path, whether he be an old person abandoned by all, a foreign laborer unjustly looked down upon, a refugee, a child born of an unlawful union and wrongly suffering for a sin he did not commit, or a hungry person who disturbs our conscience by recalling the voice of the Lord, "As long as you did it for one of these the least of my brethren, you did it for me" (Matt. 25:40).

Furthermore, whatever is opposed to life itself, such as any type of murder, genocide, abortion, euthanasia or wilful self-destruction, whatever violates the integrity of the human person, such as mutilation, torments inflicted on body or mind, attempts to coerce the will itself; whatever insults human dignity, such as subhuman living conditions, arbitrary imprisonment, deportation, slavery, prostitution, the selling of women and children; as well as disgraceful working conditions, where men are treated as mere tools for profit, rather than as free and responsible persons; all these things and others of their like are infamies indeed. They poison human society, but they do more harm to those who practice them

25

than those who suffer from the injury. Moreover, they are a supreme dishonor to the Creator.

28.   Respect and love ought to be extended also to those who think or act differently than we do in social, political and even religious matters. In fact, the more deeply we come to understand their ways of thinking through such courtesy and love, the more easily will we be able to enter into dialogue with them.

This love and good will, to be sure, must in no way render us indifferent to truth and goodness. Indeed love itself impels the disciples of Christ to speak the saving truth to all men. But it is necessary to distinguish between error, which always merits repudiation, and the person in error, who never loses the dignity of being a person even when he is flawed by false or inadequate religious notions.[10] God alone is the judge and searcher of hearts; for that reason He forbids us to make judgments about the internal guilt of anyone.[11]

The teaching of Christ even requires that we forgive injuries,[12] and extends the law of love to include every enemy, according to the command of the New Law: "You have heard that it was said: Thou shalt love thy neighbor and hate thy enemy. But I say to you: love your enemies, do good to those who hate you, and pray for those who persecute and calumniate you" (Matt. 5:43, 44).

29.   Since all men possess a rational soul and are created in God's likeness, since they have the same nature and origin, have been redeemed by Christ and enjoy the same divine calling and destiny, the basic equality of all must receive increasingly greater recognition.

True, all men are not alike from the point of view of varying physical power and the diversity of intellectual and moral resources. Nevertheless, with respect to the fundamental rights of the person, every type of discrimination, whether social or cultural, whether based on sex, race, color, social condition, language or religion, is to be overcome and eradicated as contrary to God's intent. For in truth it must still be regretted that fundamental personal rights are not yet being universally honored. Such is the case of a woman who is denied the right to choose a husband freely, to embrace a state of life or to acquire an education or cultural benefits equal to those recognized for men.

Therefore, although rightful differences exist between men, the equal dignity of persons demands that a more humane and a just condition of life be brought about. For excessive economic and social differences between the members of the one human family or population groups cause scandal, and militate against social justice, equity, the dignity of the human person, as well as social and international peace.

Human institutions, both private and public, must labor to minister to the dignity and purpose of man. At the same time let them put up a stubborn fight against any kind of slavery, whether social or political, and safeguard the basic rights of man under every political system. Indeed human institutions themselves must be accommodated by degrees to the highest of all realities, spiritual ones, even though meanwhile, a long enough time will be required before they arrive at the desired goal.

30. Profound and rapid changes make it more necessary that no one ignoring the trend of events or drugged by laziness, content himself with a merely individualistic morality. It becomes increasingly true that the obligations of justice and love are fulfilled only if each person, contributing to the common good, according to his own abilities and the needs of others, also promotes and assists the public and private institutions dedicated to bettering the conditions of human life. Yet there are those who, while professing grand and rather noble sentiments, nevertheless in reality live always as if they cared nothing for the needs of society. Many in various places even make light of social laws and precepts, and do not hesitate to resort to various frauds and deceptions in avoiding just taxes or other debts due to society. Others think little of certain norms of social life, for example those designed for the protection of health, or laws establishing speed limits; they do not even avert to the fact that by such indifference they imperil their own life and that of others.

27

Let everyone consider it his sacred obligation to esteem and observe social necessities as being among the primary duties of modern man. For the more unified the world becomes, the more plainly do the offices of men extend beyond particular groups and spread by degrees to the whole world. But this development cannot occur unless individual men and their associations cultivate in themselves the moral and social virtues, and promote them in society; thus, with the needed help of divine grace men who are truly new and artisans of a new humanity can be forthcoming.

31. Individual men, in order to discharge with greater exactness the obligations of their conscience toward themselves and the various groups to which they belong, must be carefully educated to a higher degree of culture through the use of the immense resources available today to the human race. Above all the education of youth from every social background has to be undertaken, so that there can be produced not only men and women of refined talents, but those great-souled persons who are so desperately required by our times.

Now a man can scarcely arrive at the needed sense of responsibility, unless his living conditions allow him to become conscious of his dignity, and to rise to his destiny by spending himself for God and for others. But human freedom is often crippled when a man encounters extreme poverty, just as it withers when he indulges in too many of life's comforts and imprisons himself in a kind of splendid isolation. Freedom acquires new strength, by contrast, when a man consents to the unavoidable requirements of social life, takes on the manifold demands of human partnership, and commits himself to the service of the human community.

Hence, the will to play one's role in common endeavors should be everywhere encouraged. Praise is due to those national processes which allow the largest possible number of citizens to participate in public affairs with genuine freedom. Account must be taken, to be sure, of the actual conditions of each people and the firmness required by public authority. If every citizen is to feel inclined to take part in the activities of the various groups which make up the social body, these must offer advantages which will attract members and dispose them to serve others. We can justly consider that the future of humanity lies in the hands of those who are strong enough to provide coming generations with reasons for living and hoping.

32.   As God did not create man for life in isolation, but for the formation of social unity, so also "it has pleased God to make men holy and save them not merely as individuals, without bond or link between them, but by making them into a single people, a people which acknowledges Him in truth and serves Him in holiness".[13] So from the beginning of salvation history He has chosen men not just as individuals but as members of a certain community. Revealing His mind to them, God called these chosen ones "His people" (Ex. 3:7, 12), and even made a covenant with them on Sinai.[14]

This communitarian character is developed and consummated in the work of Jesus Christ. For the very Word made flesh willed to share in the human fellowship. He was present at the wedding of Cana, visited the house of Zachaeus, ate with publicans and sinners. He revealed the love of the Father and the sublime vocation of man in terms of the most common of social realities and by making use of the speech and the imagery of plain everyday life. Willingly obeying the laws of His country, / He sanctified those human ties, especially family ones, which are the foundation of social structures. He chose to lead the life proper to an artisan of His time and place.

In His preaching He clearly taught the sons of God to treat one another as brothers. In His prayers He pleaded that all His disciples might be "one." Indeed as the Redeemer of all, He offered Himself for all even to the point of death. "Greater love than this no one has, that one lay down his life for his friends" (John 15:13). He commanded His Apostles to preach to all peoples the Gospel's message that the human race was to become the Family of God, in which the fullness of the Law would be love.

As the firstborn of many brethren and by the giving of His Spirit, He founded after His death and resurrection a new brotherly community composed of all those who receive Him in faith and in

29

love. This He did through His Body, which is the Church. There everyone, as members one of the other, would render mutual service according to the different gifts bestowed on each.

This solidarity must be constantly increased until that day on which it will be brought to perfection. Then, saved by grace, men will offer flawless glory to God as a family beloved of God and of Christ their Brother.

CHAPTER III

MAN'S ACTIVITY
THROUGHOUT
THE WORLD

33. Through his labors and his native endowments man has ceaselessly striven to better his life. Today, however, especially with the help of science and technology, he has extended his mastery over nearly the whole of nature and continues to do so. Thanks to increased opportunities for many kinds of social contact among nations, the human family is gradually recognizing that it comprises a single world community and is making itself so. Hence many benefits once looked for, especially from heavenly powers, man has now enterprisingly procured for himself.

In the face of these immense efforts which already preoccupy the whole human race, men raise numerous questions among themselves. What is the meaning and value of this feverish activity? How should all these things be used? To the achievement of what goal are the strivings of individuals and societies heading? The Church guards the heritage of God's Word and draws from it moral and religious principles without always having at hand the solution to particular problems. As such she desires to add the light of revealed truth to mankind's store of experience, so that the path which humanity has taken in recent times will not be a dark one.

34. Throughout the course of the centuries, men have labored to better the circumstances of their lives through a monumental amount of individual and collective effort. To believers, this point is settled: considered in itself, this human activity accords with God's will. For man, created to God's image, received a mandate

to subject to himself the earth and all it contains, and to govern the world with justice and holiness;[1] a mandate to relate himself and the totality of things to Him Who was to be acknowledged as the Lord and Creator of all. Thus, by the subjection of all things to man, the name of God would be wonderful in all the earth.[2]

This mandate concerns the whole range of everyday activity as well. For while providing the substance of life for themselves and their families, men and women are performing their activities in a way which appropriately benefits society. They can justly consider that by their labor they are unfolding the Creator's work, consulting the advantages of their brother men, and are contributing by their personal industry to the realization in history of the divine plan.[3]

Thus, far from thinking that works produced by man's own talent and energy are in opposition to God's power, and that the rational creature exists as a kind of rival to the Creator, Christians are convinced that the triumphs of the human race are a sign of God's grace and the flowering of His own mysterious design. For the greater man's power becomes, the further his individual and community responsibility extends. Hence it is clear that men are not deterred by the Christian message from building up the world, or impelled to neglect the welfare of their fellows, but that they are rather more stringently bound to do these very things.[4]

35.   Human activity, to be sure, takes its significance from its relationship to man. Just as it proceeds from man, so it is ordered toward man. For when a man works he not only alters things and society, he develops himself as well. He learns much, he cultivates his resources, he goes outside of himself and beyond himself. Rightly understood, this kind of growth is of greater value than any external riches which can be garnered. A man is more precious for what he is than for what he has.[5] Similarly, all that men do to obtain greater justice, wider brotherhood, a more humane ordering of social relationships has greater worth than technical advances. For these advances can supply the material for human progress, but of themselves alone they can never actually bring it about.

Hence, the norm of human activity is this: that in accord with the divine plan and will, it harmonize with the genuine good of the human race, and that it allow men as individuals and as members of society to pursue their total vocation and fulfil it.

36. Now many of our contemporaries seem to fear that a closer bond between human activity and religion will work against the independence of men, of societies, or of the sciences.

If by the autonomy of earthly affairs we mean that created things and societies themselves enjoy their own laws and values which must be gradually deciphered, put to use, and regulated by men, then it is entirely right to demand that autonomy. This is not merely required by modern man, but harmonizes also with the will of the Creator. For by the very circumstance of their having been created, all things are endowed with their own stability, truth, goodness, proper laws and order. Man must respect these as he isolates them by the appropriate methods of the individual sciences or arts. Therefore if methodical investigation within every branch of learning is carried out in a genuinely scientific manner and in accord with moral norms, it never truly conflicts with faith, for earthly matters and the concerns of faith derive from the same God.[6] Indeed whoever labors to penetrate the secrets of reality with a humble and steady mind, even though he is unaware of the fact, is nevertheless being led by the hand of God, Who holds all things in existence, and gives them their identity. Consequently, we cannot but deplore certain habits of mind, which are sometimes found too among Christians, which do not sufficiently attend to the rightful independence of science and which, from the arguments and controversies they spark, lead many minds to conclude that faith and science are mutually opposed.[7]

But if the expression, the autonomy of temporal affairs, is taken to mean that created things do not depend on God, and that man can use them without any reference to their Creator, anyone who acknowledges God will see how false such a meaning is. For without the Creator the creature would disappear. For their part, however, all believers of whatever religion always hear His revealing

33

voice in the discourse of creatures. When God is forgotten, however, the creature itself grows unintelligible.

37. Sacred Scripture teaches the human family what the experience of the ages confirms: that while human progress is a great advantage to man, it brings with it a strong temptation. For when the order of values is jumbled and bad is mixed with the good, individuals and groups pay heed solely to their own interests, and not to those of others. Thus it happens that the world ceases to be a place of true brotherhood. In our own day, the magnified power of humanity threatens to destroy the race itself.

For a monumental struggle against the powers of darkness pervades the whole history of man. The battle was joined from the very origins of the world and will continue until the last day, as the Lord has attested.[8] Caught in this conflict, man is obliged to wrestle constantly if he is to cling to what is good, nor can he achieve his own integrity without great efforts and the help of God's grace.

That is why Christ's Church, trusting in the design of the Creator, acknowledges that human progress can serve man's true happiness, yet she cannot help echoing the Apostle's warning: "Be not conformed to this world" (Rom. 12:2). Here by the world is meant that spirit of vanity and malice which transforms into an instrument of sin those human energies intended for the service of God and man.

Hence if anyone wants to know how this unhappy situation can be overcome, Christians will tell him that all human activity, constantly imperiled by man's pride and deranged self-love, must be purified and perfected by the power of Christ's Cross and resurrection. For redeemed by Christ and made a new creature in the Holy Spirit, man is able to love the things themselves created by God, and ought to do so. He can receive them from God and respect and reverence them as flowing constantly from the hand of God. Grateful to his Benefactor for these creatures, using and enjoying them in detachment and liberty of spirit, man is led forward into a true possession of them, as having nothing, yet possessing all things.[9] "All are yours, and you are Christ's, and Christ is God's" (I Cor. 3:22-23).

38. For God's Word, through Whom all things were made, was Himself made flesh and dwelt on man's earth.[10] Thus He entered the world's history as a perfect man, taking that history up into Himself and summarizing it.[11] He Himself revealed to us that "God is love" (I John 4:8) and at the same time taught us that the new command of love was the basic law of human perfection and hence of the world's transformation.

To those, therefore, who believe in divine love, He gives assurance that the way of love lies open to men and that the effort to establish a universal brotherhood is not a hopeless one. He cautions them at the same time that this love is not something to be reserved for important matters, but must be pursued chiefly in the ordinary circumstances of life. Undergoing death itself for all of us sinners,[12] He taught us by example that we too must shoulder that cross which the world and the flesh inflict upon those who search after peace and justice. Appointed Lord by His resurrection and given all power in heaven and on earth,[13] Christ is now at work in the hearts of men through the energy of His Spirit, arousing not only a desire for the age to come, but by that very fact animating, purifying and strengthening those noble longings too by which the human family makes its life more human and strives to render the whole earth submissive to this goal.

Now, the gifts of the Spirit are diverse: while He calls some to give clear witness to the desire for a heavenly home and to keep that desire fresh among the human family, He summons others to dedicate themselves to the earthly service of men and to make ready the material of the celestial realm by this ministry of theirs. Yet He frees all of them so that by putting aside love of self and bringing all earthly resources into the service of human life they can devote themselves to that future when humanity itself will become an offering accepted by God.[14]

The Lord left behind a pledge of this hope and strength for life's journey in that sacrament of faith where natural elements refined by man are gloriously changed into His Body and Blood, providing a meal of brotherly solidarity and a foretaste of the heavenly banquet.

39. We do not know the time for the consummation of the earth and of humanity,[15] nor do we know how all things will be transformed. As deformed by sin, the shape of this world will pass away;[16] but we are taught that God is preparing a new dwelling place and a new earth where justice will abide,[17] and whose blessedness will answer and surpass all the longings for peace which spring up in the human heart.[18] Then, with death overcome, the sons of God will be raised up in Christ, and what was sown in weakness and corruption will be clothed with incorruptibility.[19] Enduring with charity and its fruits,[20] all that creation[21] which God made on man's account will be unchained from the bondage of vanity.

Therefore, while we are warned that it profits a man nothing if he gain the whole world and lose himself,[22] the expectation of a new earth must not weaken but rather stimulate our concern for cultivating this one. For here grows the body of a new human family, a body which even now is able to give some kind of foreshadowing of the new age.

Hence, while earthly progress must be carefully distinguished from the growth of Christ's Kingdom, to the extent that the former can contribute to the better ordering of human society, it is of vital concern to the Kingdom of God.[23]

For after we have obeyed the Lord, and in His Spirit nurtured on earth the values of human dignity, brotherhood and freedom, and indeed all the good fruits of our nature and enterprise, we will find them again, but freed of stain, burnished and transfigured, when Christ hands over to the Father: "a kingdom eternal and universal, a kingdom of truth and life, of holiness and grace, of justice, love and peace."[24] On this earth that Kingdom is already present in mystery. When the Lord returns it will be brought into full flower.

CHAPTER IV

THE ROLE OF THE CHURCH IN THE MODERN WORLD

40. Everything we have said about the dignity of the human person, and about the human community and the profound meaning of human activity, lays the foundation for the relationship between the Church and the world, and provides the basis for dialogue between them.[1] In this chapter, presupposing everything which has already been said by this Council concerning the mystery of the Church, we must now consider this same Church inasmuch as she exists in the world, living and acting with it.

Coming forth from the eternal Father's love,[2] founded in time by Christ the Redeemer and made one in the Holy Spirit,[3] the Church has a saving and an eschatological purpose which can be fully attained only in the future world. But she is already present in this world, and is composed of men, that is, of members of the earthly city who have a call to form the family of God's children during the present history of the human race, and to keep increasing it until the Lord returns. United on behalf of heavenly values and enriched by them, this family has been "constituted and structured as a society in this world"[4] by Christ, and is equipped "by appropriate means for visible and social union."[5] Thus the Church, at once "a visible association and a spiritual community,"[6] goes forward together with humanity and experiences the same earthly lot which the world does. She serves as a leaven and as a kind of soul for human society[7] as it is to be renewed in Christ and transformed into God's family.

That the earthly and the heavenly city penetrate each other is a fact accessible to faith alone; it remains a mystery of human history, which sin will keep in great disarray until the splendor of God's sons is fully revealed. Pursuing the saving purpose which is proper to her, the Church does not only communicate divine life to men but in some way casts the reflected light of that life over the entire earth, most of all by its healing and elevating impact on the dignity of the person, by the way in which it strengthens the seams of human society and imbues the everyday activity of men with a deeper meaning and importance. Thus through her individual members and her whole community, the Church believes she can contribute greatly toward making the family of man and its history more human.

In addition, the Catholic Church gladly holds in high esteem the things which other Christian Churches and ecclesial communities have done or are doing cooperatively by way of achieving the same goal. At the same time, she is convinced that she can be abundantly and variously helped by the world in the matter of preparing the ground for the Gospel. This help she gains from the talents and industry of individuals and from human society as a whole. The Council now sets forth certain general principles for the proper fostering of this mutual exchange and assistance in concerns which are in some way common to the world and the Church.

41. Modern man is on the road to a more thorough development of his own personality, and to a growing discovery and vindication of his own rights. Since it has been entrusted to the Church to reveal the mystery of God, Who is the ultimate goal of man, she opens up to man at the same time the meaning of his own existence, that is, the innermost truth about himself. The Church truly knows that only God, Whom she serves, meets the deepest longings of the human heart, which is never fully satisfied by what this world has to offer.

She also knows that man is constantly worked upon by God's Spirit, and hence can never be altogether indifferent to the problems of religion. The experience of past ages proves this, as do numerous indications in our own times. For man will always yearn to know, at least in an obscure way, what is the meaning of his life, of his activity, of his death. The very presence of the Church recalls these problems to his mind. But only God, Who created man to His own image and ransomed him from sin, provides a fully adequate answer to these questions, and this He does through what He has revealed in Christ His Son, Who became man. Whoever follows after Christ, the perfect man, becomes himself more of a man. For by His incarnation the Father's Word assumed, and sanctified through His cross and resurrection, the whole of man, body and soul, and through that totality the whole of nature created by God for man's use.

Thanks to this belief, the Church can anchor the dignity of human nature against all tides of opinion, for example those which undervalue the human body or idolize it. By no human law can the personal dignity and liberty of man be so aptly safeguarded as by the Gospel of Christ which has been entrusted to the Church. For this Gospel announces and proclaims the freedom of the sons of God, and repudiates all the bondage which ultimately results from sin (cf. Rom. 8:14-17);[8] it has a sacred reverence for the dignity of conscience and its freedom of choice, constantly advises that all human talents be employed in God's service and men's, and, finally, commends all to the charity of all (cf. Matt. 22:39).[9]

This agrees with the basic law of the Christian dispensation. For though the same God is Saviour and Creator, Lord of human history as well as of salvation history, in the divine arrangement itself, the rightful autonomy of the creature, and particularly of man is not withdrawn, but is rather re-established in its own dignity and strengthened in it.

The Church, therefore, by virtue of the Gospel committed to her, proclaims the rights of man; she acknowledges and greatly esteems the dynamic movements of today by which these rights are everywhere fostered. Yet these movements must be penetrated by the spirit of the Gospel and protected against any kind of false autonomy. For we are tempted to think that our personal rights are fully ensured only when we are exempt from every requirement of divine law. But this way lies not the maintenance of the dignity of the human person, but its annihilation.

42. The union of the human family is greatly fortified and fulfilled by the unity, founded on Christ,[10] of the family of God's sons.

Christ, to be sure, gave His Church no proper mission in the political, economic or social order. The purpose which He set before her is a religious one.[11] But out of this religious mission itself come a function, a light and an energy which can serve to structure and consolidate the human community according to the divine law. As a matter of fact, when circumstances of time and place produce the need, she can and indeed should initiate activities on behalf of all men, especially those designed for the needy, such as the works of mercy and similar undertakings.

The Church recognizes that worthy elements are found in today's social movements, especially an evolution toward unity, a process of wholesome socialization and of association in civic and economic realms. The promotion of unity belongs to the innermost nature of the Church, for she is, "thanks to her relationship with Christ, a sacramental sign and an instrument of intimate union with God, and of the unity of the whole human race."[12] Thus she shows the world that an authentic union, social and external, results from a union of minds and hearts, namely from that faith and charity by which her own unity is unbreakably rooted in the Holy Spirit. For the force which the Church can inject into the modern society of man consists in that faith and charity put into vital practice, not in any external dominion exercised by merely human means.

Moreover, since in virtue of her mission and nature she is bound to no particular form of human culture, nor to any political, economic or social system, the Church by her very universality can be a very close bond between diverse human communities and nations, provided these trust her and truly acknowledge her right to true freedom in fulfilling her mission. For this reason, the Church admonishes her own sons, but also humanity as a whole, to overcome all strife between nations and races in this family spirit of God's children, and in the same way, to give internal strength to human associations which are just.

Therefore, this Council regards with great respect all the true, good and just elements inherent in the very wide variety of institutions which the human race has established for itself and constantly continues to establish. The Council affirms, moreover, that the Church is willing to assist and promote all these institutions to the extent that such a service depends on her and can be associated with her mission. She has no fiercer desire than that in pursuit of the welfare of all she may be able to develop herself freely under any kind of government which grants recognition to the basic rights of person and family, to the demands of the common good and to the free exercise of her own mission.

43. This Council exhorts Christians, as citizens of two cities, to strive to discharge their earthly duties conscientiously and in response to the Gospel spirit. They are mistaken who, knowing that we have here no abiding city but seek one which is to come,[18] think that they may therefore shirk their earthly responsibilities. For they are forgetting that by the faith itself they are more obliged than ever to measure up to these duties, each according to his proper vocation.[14] Nor, on the contrary, are they any less wide of the mark who think that religion consists in acts of worship alone and in the discharge of certain moral obligations, and who imagine they can plunge themselves into earthly affairs in such a way as to imply that these are altogether divorced from the religious life. This split between the faith which many profess and their daily lives deserves to be counted among the more serious errors of our age. Long since, the Prophets of the Old Testament fought vehemently against this scandal[15] and even more so did Jesus Christ Himself in the New Testament threaten it with grave punishments.[16] Therefore, let there be no false opposition between professional and social activities on the one part, and religious life on the other. The Christian who neglects his temporal duties, neglects his duties toward his neighbor and even God, and jeopardizes his eternal salvation. Christians should rather rejoice that, following the example of Christ Who worked as an artisan, they are free to exercise all their earthly activities by gathering their humane,

domestic, professional, social and technical enterprises into one vital synthesis with religious values, under whose supreme direction all things are harmonized unto God's glory.

Secular duties and activities belong properly although not exclusively to laymen. Therefore acting as citizens in the world, whether individually or socially, they will observe the laws proper to each discipline, and labor to equip themselves with a genuine expertise in their various fields. They will gladly work with men seeking the same goals. Acknowledging the demands of faith and endowed with its force, they will unhesitatingly devise new enterprises, where they are appropriate, and put them into action. Laymen should also know that it is generally the function of their well-formed Christian conscience to see that the divine law is inscribed in the life of the earthly city; from priests they may look for spiritual light and nourishment. Let the layman not imagine that his pastors are always such experts, that to every problem which arises, however complicated, they can readily give him a concrete solution, or even that such is their mission Rather, enlightened by Christian wisdom and giving close attention to the teaching authority of the Church,[17] let the layman take on his own distinctive role.

Often enough the Christian view of things will itself suggest some specific solution in certain circumstances. Yet it happens rather frequently, and legitimately so, that with equal sincerity some of the faithful will disagree with others on a given matter. Even against the intentions of their proponents, however, solutions proposed on one side or another may be easily confused by many people with the Gospel message. Hence it is necessary for people to remember that no one is allowed in the aforementioned situations to appropriate the Church's authority for his opinion. They should always try to enlighten one another through honest discussion, preserving mutual charity and caring above all for the common good.

Since they have an active role to play in the whole life of the Church, laymen are not only bound to penetrate the world with a Christian spirit, but are also called to be witnesses to Christ in all things in the midst of human society.

Bishops, to whom is assigned the task of ruling the Church of God, should, together with their priests, so preach the news of Christ that all the earthly activities of the faithful will be bathed in the light of the Gospel. All pastors should remember too that by their daily conduct and concern[18] they are revealing the face of the Church to the world, and men will judge the power and truth of the Christian message thereby. By their lives and speech, in union with Religious and their faithful, may they demonstrate that even now the Church, by her presence alone and by all the gifts which she contains, is an unspent fountain of those virtues which the modern world needs the most.

By unremitting study they should fit themselves to do their part in establishing dialogue with the world and with men of all shades of opinion. Above all let them take to heart the words which this Council has spoken: "Since humanity today increasingly moves toward civil, economic and social unity, it is more than ever necessary that priests, with joint concern and energy, and under the guidance of the bishops and the supreme pontiff, erase every cause of division, so that the whole human race may be led to the unity of God's family."[19]

Although by the power of the Holy Spirit the Church will remain the faithful spouse of her Lord and will never cease to be the sign of salvation on earth, still she is very well aware that among her members,[20] both clerical and lay, some have been unfaithful to the Spirit of God during the course of many centuries; in the present age, too, it does not escape the Church how great a distance lies between the message she offers and the human failings of those to whom the Gospel is entrusted. Whatever be the judgment of history on these defects, we ought to be conscious of them, and struggle against them energetically, lest they inflict harm on spread of the Gospel. The Church also realizes that in working out her relationship with the world she always has great need of the ripening which comes with the experience of the centuries. Led by the Holy Spirit, Mother Church unceasingly exhorts her sons "to purify and renew themselves so that the sign of Christ can shine more brightly on the face of the Church."[21]

44. Just as it is in the world's interest to acknowledge the Church as a historical reality, and to recognize her good influence, so the Church herself knows how richly she has profited by the history and development of humanity.

The experience of past ages, the progress of the sciences, and the treasures hidden in the various forms of human culture, by all of which the nature of man himself is more clearly revealed and new roads to truth are opened, these profit the Church, too. For, from the beginning of her history she has learned to express the message of Christ with the help of the ideas and terminology of various philosophers, and has tried to clarify it with their wisdom, too. Her purpose has been to adapt the Gospel to the grasp of all as well as to the needs of the learned, insofar as such was appropriate. Indeed this accommodated preaching of the revealed Word ought to remain the law of all evangelization. For thus the ability to express Christ's message in its own way is developed in each nation, and at the same time there is fostered a living exchange between the Church and the diverse cultures of people.[22] To promote such exchange, especially in our days, the Church requires the special help of those who live in the world, are versed in different institutions and specialties, and grasp their innermost significance in the eyes of both believers and unbelievers. With the help of the Holy Spirit, it is the task of the entire People of God, especially pastors and theologians, to hear, distinguish and interpret the many voices of our age, and to judge them in the light of the divine Word, so that revealed truth can always be more deeply penetrated, better understood and set forth to greater advantage.

Since the Church has a visible and social structure as a sign of her unity in Christ, she can and ought to be enriched by the development of human social life, not that there is any lack in the constitution given her by Christ, but that she can understand it more penetratingly, express it better, and adjust it more successfully to our times. Moreover, she gratefully understands that in her community life no less than in her individual sons, she receives a variety of helps from men of every rank and condition, for whoever promotes the human community at the family level, culturally, in its eco-

nomic, social and political dimensions, both nationally and inter-
nationally, such a one, according to God's design, is contributing
greatly to the Church as well, to the extent that she depends on
things outside herself. Indeed, the Church admits that she has
greatly profited and still profits from the antagonism of those who
oppose or who persecute her.[23]

45. While helping the world and receiving many benefits
from it, the Church has a single intention: that God's Kingdom may
come, and that the salvation of the whole human race may come to
pass. For every benefit which the People of God during its earthly
pilgrimage can offer to the human family stems from the fact that
the Church is "the universal sacrament of salvation",[24] simultaneously manifesting and exercising the mystery of God's love for man.

For God's Word, by Whom all things were made, was Himself
made flesh so that as perfect man He might save all men and sum
up all things in Himself. The Lord is the goal of human history,
the focal point of the longings of history and of civilization, the
center of the human race, the joy of every heart and the answer
to all its yearnings.[25] He it is Whom the Father raised from the
dead, lifted on high and stationed at His right hand, making Him
judge of the living and the dead. Enlivened and united in His Spirit,
we journey toward the consummation of human history, one which
fully accords with the counsel of God's love: "To re-establish all
things in Christ, both those in the heavens and those on the earth"
(Eph. 11:10).

The Lord Himself speaks: "Behold I come quickly! And my
reward is with me, to render to each one according to his works.
I am the Alpha and the Omega, the first and the last, the beginning
and the end" (Apoc. 22:12-13).

PART II:

SOME PROBLEMS
OF SPECIAL URGENCY

46. This Council has set forth the dignity of the human person, and the work which men have been destined to undertake throughout the world both as individuals and as members of society. There are a number of particularly urgent needs characterizing the present age, needs which go to the roots of the human race. To a consideration of these in the light of the Gospel and of human experience, the Council would now direct the attention of all.

Of the many subjects arousing universal concern today, it may be helpful to concentrate on these: marriage and the family, human progress, life in its economic, social and political dimensions, the bonds between the family of nations, and peace. On each of these may there shine the radiant ideals proclaimed by Christ. By these ideals may Christians be led, and all mankind enlightened, as they search for answers to questions of such complexity.

CHAPTER I

FOSTERING THE NOBILITY
OF MARRIAGE
AND THE FAMILY

47.   The well-being of the individual person and of human and Christian society is intimately linked with the healthy condition of that community produced by marriage and family.   Hence Christians and all men who hold this community in high esteem sincerely rejoice in the various ways by which men today find help in fostering this community of love and perfecting its life, and by which parents are assisted in their lofty calling.   Those who rejoice in such aids look for additional benefits from them and labor to bring them about.

Yet the excellence of this institution is not everywhere reflected with equal brilliance, since polygamy, the plague of divorce, so-called free love and other disfigurements have an obscuring effect.   In addition, married love is too often profaned by excessive self-love, the worship of pleasure and illicit practices against human generation.   Moreover, serious disturbances are caused in families by modern economic conditions, by influences at once social and psychological, and by the demands of civil society.   Finally, in certain parts of the world problems resulting from population growth are generating concern.

All these situations have produced anxiety of conscience.   Yet, the power and strength of the institution of marriage and family can also be seen in the fact that time and again, despite the difficulties produced, the profound changes in modern society reveal the true character of this institution in one way or another.

Therefore, by presenting certain key points of Church doctrine in a clearer light, this sacred Synod wishes to offer guidance and support to those Christians and other men who are trying to preserve the holiness and to foster the natural dignity of the married state and its superlative value.

48. The intimate partnership of married life and love has been established by the Creator and qualified by His laws, and is rooted in the conjugal covenant of irrevocable personal consent. Hence by that human act whereby spouses mutually bestow and accept each other a relationship arises which by divine will and in the eyes of society too is a lasting one. For the good of the spouses and their offspring as well as of society, the existence of the sacred bond no longer depends on human decisions alone. For God Himself is the author of matrimony, endowed as it is with various benefits and purposes.[1] All of these have a very decisive bearing on the continuation of the human race, on the personal development and eternal destiny of the individual members of a family, and on the dignity, stability, peace and prosperity of the family itself and of human society as a whole. By their very nature, the institution of matrimony itself and conjugal love are ordained for the procreation and education of children, and find in them their ultimate crown. Thus a man and a woman, who by their compact of conjugal love "are no longer two, but one flesh" (Matt. 19:6), render mutual help and service to each other through an intimate union of their persons and of their actions. Through this union they experience the meaning of their oneness and attain to it with growing perfection day by day. As a mutual gift of two persons, this intimate union and the good of the children impose total fidelity on the spouses and argue for an unbreakable oneness between them.[2]

Christ the Lord abundantly blessed this many-faceted love, welling up as it does from the fountain of divine love and structured as it is on the model of His union with His Church. For as God of old made Himself present[3] to His people through a covenant of love and fidelity, so now the Saviour of men and the Spouse[4] of the Church comes into the lives of married Christians through the Sacrament of Matrimony. He abides with them thereafter so that, just as He loved the Church and handed Himself over on her behalf,[5] the spouses may love each other with perpetual fidelity through mutual self-bestowal.

Authentic married love is caught up into divine love and is governed and enriched by Christ's redeeming power and the saving activity of the Church, so that this love may lead the spouses to God with powerful effect and may aid and strengthen them in the sublime office of being a father or a mother.[6] For this reason Christian spouses have a special sacrament by which they are fortified and receive a kind of consecration in the duties and dignity of their state.[7] By virtue of this sacrament, as spouses fulfill their conjugal and family obligations, they are penetrated with the spirit of Christ, which suffuses their whole lives with faith, hope and charity. Thus they increasingly advance the perfection of their own personalities, as well as their mutual sanctification, and hence contribute jointly to the glory of God.

As a result, with their parents leading the way by example and family prayer, children and indeed everyone gathered around the family hearth will find a readier path to human maturity, salvation and holiness. Graced with the dignity and office of fatherhood and motherhood, parents will energetically acquit themselves of a duty which devolves primarily on them, namely education and especially religious education.

As living members of the family, children contribute in their own way to making their parents holy. For they will respond to the kindness of their parents with sentiments of gratitude, with love and trust. They will stand by them as children should when hardships overtake their parents and old age brings its loneliness. Widowhood, accepted bravely as a continuation of the marriage vocation, should be esteemed by all.[8] Families too will share their spiritual riches generously with other families. Thus the Christian family, which springs from marriage as a reflection of the loving covenant uniting Christ with the Church,[9] and as a participation in that covenant, will manifest to all men Christ's living presence in the world, and the genuine nature of the Church. This the family will do by the mutual love of the spouses, by their generous fruitfulness, their solidarity and faithfulness, and by the loving way in which all members of the family assist one another.

49.   The biblical Word of God several times urges the betrothed and the married to nourish and develop their wedlock by pure conjugal love and undivided affection.[10] Many men of our own age also highly regard true love between husband and wife as it manifests itself in a variety of ways depending on the worthy customs of various peoples and times.

This love is an eminently human one since it is directed from one person to another through an affection of the will; it involves the good of the whole person, and therefore can enrich the expressions of the body and mind with a unique dignity, ennobling these expressions as special ingredients and signs of the friendship distinctive of marriage. This love God has judged worthy of special gifts, healing, perfecting and exalting gifts of grace and of charity. Such love, merging the human with the divine, leads the spouses to a free and mutual gift of themselves, a gift proving itself by gentle affection and by deed; such love pervades the whole of their lives:[11] indeed by its active generosity it grows better and grows greater. Therefore it far excels mere erotic inclination, which, selfishly pursued, soon enough fades wretchedly away.

This love is uniquely expressed and perfected in the special area of matrimony. The actions within marriage by which the couple are united intimately and chastely are noble and worthy ones. Expressed in a manner which is truly human, these actions promote that mutual self-giving by which spouses enrich each other with a joyful and a ready will. Sealed by mutual faithfulness and hallowed above all by Christ's sacrament, this love remains steadfastly true in body and in mind, in bright days or dark. It will never be profaned by adultery or divorce. Firmly established by the Lord, the unity of marriage will radiate from the equal personal dignity of wife and husband, a dignity acknowledged by mutual and total love. The constant fulfilment of the duties of this Christian vocation demands notable virtue. For this reason, strengthened by grace for holiness of life, the couple will painstakingly cultivate and pray for steadfastness of love, large-heartedness and the spirit of sacrifice.

Authentic conjugal love will be more highly prized, and wholesome public opinion created regarding it if Christian couples give outstanding witness to faithfulness and harmony in their love, and to their concern for educating their children; also, if they do their part in bringing about the needed cultural, psychological and social renewal on behalf of marriage and the family. Especially in the heart of their own families, young people should be aptly and seasonably instructed in the dignity, duty and work of married love. Trained thus in the cultivation of chastity, they will be able at a suitable age to enter a marriage of their own after an honorable courtship.

50.   Marriage and conjugal love are by their nature ordained toward the begetting and educating of children. Children are really the supreme gift of marriage and contribute very substantially to the welfare of their parents. The God Himself Who said, "it is not good for man to be alone" (Gen. 2:18) and "Who made man from the beginning male and female" (Matt. 19:4); wishing to share with man a certain special participation in His own creative work, blessed male and female, saying: "Increase and multiply" (Gen. 1:28). Hence, while not making the other purposes of matrimony of less account, the true practice of conjugal love, and the whole meaning of the family life which results from it, have this aim: that the couple be ready with stout hearts to cooperate with the love of the Creator and the Saviour, Who through them will enlarge and enrich His own family day by day.

Parents should regard as their proper mission the task of transmitting human life and educating those to whom it has been transmitted. They should realize that they are thereby cooperators with the love of God the Creator, and are, so to speak, the interpreters of that love. Thus they will fulfill their task with human and Christian responsibility, and, with docile reverence toward God, will make decisions by common counsel and effort. Let them

51

thoughtfully take into account both their own welfare and that of their children, those already born and those which the future may bring. For this accounting they need to reckon with both the material and the spiritual conditions of the times as well as of their state in life. Finally, they should consult the interests of the family group, of temporal society, and of the Church herself. The parents themselves should ultimately make this judgment in the sight of God. But in their manner of acting, spouses should be aware that they cannot proceed arbitrarily, but must always be governed according to a conscience dutifully conformed to the divine law itself, and should be submissive toward the Church's teaching office, which authentically interprets that law in the light of the Gospel. That divine law reveals and protects the integral meaning of conjugal love, and impels it toward a truly human fulfilment. Thus, trusting in divine Providence and refining the spirit of sacrifice,[12] married Christians glorify the Creator and strive toward fulfilment in Christ when with a generous human and Christian sense of responsibility they acquit themselves of the duty to procreate. Among the couples who fulfil their God-given task in this way, those merit special mention who with a gallant heart, and with wise and common deliberation, undertake to bring up suitably even a relatively large family.[13]

Marriage to be sure is not instituted solely for procreation; rather, its very nature as an unbreakable compact between persons, and the welfare of the children, both demand that the mutual love of the spouses be embodied in a rightly ordered manner, that it grow and ripen. Therefore, marriage persists as a whole manner and communion of life, and maintains its value and indissolubility, even when, despite the often intense desire of the couple, offspring are lacking.

51. This Council realizes that certain modern conditions often keep couples from arranging their married lives harmoniously, and that they find themselves in circumstances where at least temporarily the size of their families should not be increased. As a result, the faithful exercise of love and the full intimacy of their

lives is hard to maintain. But where the intimacy of married life is broken off, its faithfulness can sometimes be imperiled and its quality of fruitfulness ruined, for then the upbringing of the children and the courage to accept new ones are both endangered.

To these problems there are those who presume to offer dishonorable solutions indeed; they do not recoil even from the taking of life. But the Church issues the reminder that a true contradiction cannot exist between the divine laws pertaining to the transmission of life and those pertaining to authentic conjugal love.

For God, the Lord of life, has conferred on men the surpassing ministry of safeguarding life in a manner which is worthy of man. Therefore from the moment of its conception life must be guarded with the greatest care while abortion and infanticide are unspeakable crimes. The sexual characteristics of man and the human faculty of reproduction wonderfully exceed the dispositions of lower forms of life. Hence the acts themselves which are proper to conjugal love and which are exercised in accord with genuine human dignity must be honored with great reverence. Hence when there is question of harmonizing conjugal love with the responsible transmission of life, the moral aspect of any procedure does not depend solely on sincere intentions or on an evaluation of motives, but must be determined by objective standards. These, based on the nature of the human person and his acts preserve the full sense of mutual self-giving and human procreation in the context of true love. Such a goal cannot be achieved unless the virtue of conjugal chastity is sincerely practiced. Relying on these principles, sons of the Church may not undertake methods of birth regulation which are found blameworthy by the teaching authority of the Church in its unfolding of the divine law.[14]

All should be persuaded that human life and the task of transmitting it are not realities bound up with this world alone. Hence they cannot be measured or perceived only in terms of it, but always have a bearing on the eternal destiny of men.

52. The family is a kind of school of deeper humanity. But if it is to achieve the full flowering of its life and mission, it needs the kindly communion of minds and the joint deliberation of

spouses, as well as the painstaking cooperation of parents in the education of their children. The active presence of the father is highly beneficial to their formation. The children, especially the younger among them, need the care of their mother at home. This domestic role of hers must be safely preserved, though the legitimate social progress of women should not be underrated on that account.

Children should be so educated that as adults they can follow their vocation, including a religious one, with a mature sense of responsibility and can choose their state of life; if they marry, they can thereby establish their family in favorable moral, social and economic conditions. Parents or guardians should by prudent advice provide guidance to their young with respect to founding a family, and the young ought to listen gladly. At the same time no pressure, direct or indirect, should be put on the young to make them enter marriage or choose a specific partner.

Thus the family, in which the various generations come together and help one another grow wiser and harmonize personal rights with the other requirements of social life, is the foundation of society. All those, therefore, who exercise influence over communities and social groups should work effectively for the welfare of marriage and the family. Public authority should regard it as a sacred duty to recognize, protect and promote their authentic nature, to shield public morality and to favor the prosperity of home life. The right of parents to beget and educate their children in the bosom of the family must be safeguarded. Children too who unhappily lack the blessing of a family should be protected by prudent legislation and various undertakings and assisted by the help they need.

Christians, redeeming the present time[15] and distinguishing eternal realities from their changing expressions, should actively promote the values of marriage and the family, both by the example of their own lives and by cooperation with other men of good will. Thus when difficulties arise, Christians will provide on behalf of family life those necessities and helps which are suitably modern. To this end the Christian instincts of the faithful, the upright moral consciences of men, and the wisdom and experience of persons versed in the sacred sciences will have much to contribute.

Those too who are skilled in other sciences, notably the medical, biological, social and psychological, can considerably advance the welfare of marriage and the family along with peace of conscience if by pooling their efforts they labor to explain more thoroughly the various conditions favoring a proper regulation of births.

It devolves on priests duly trained about family matters to nurture the vocation of spouses by a variety of pastoral means, by preaching God's Word, by liturgical worship, and by other spiritual aids to conjugal and family life; to sustain them sympathetically and patiently in difficulties, and to make them courageous through love, so that families which are truly illustrious can be formed.

Various organizations, especially family associations, should try by their programs of instruction and action to strengthen young people and spouses themselves, particularly those recently wed, and to train them for family, social and apostolic life.

Finally, let the spouses themselves, made to the image of the living God and enjoying the authentic dignity of persons, be joined to one another[16] in equal affection, harmony of mind and the work of mutual sanctification. Thus, following Christ who is the principle of life,[17] by the sacrifices and joys of their vocation and through their faithful love, married people can become witnesses of the mystery of love which the Lord revealed to the world by His dying and His rising up to life again.[18]

CHAPTER II

THE PROPER DEVELOPMENT
OF CULTURE

53.   Man comes to a true and full humanity only through culture, that is through the cultivation of the goods and values of nature. Wherever human life is involved, therefore, nature and culture are quite intimately connected one with the other.

The word "culture" in its general sense indicates everything whereby man develops and perfects his many bodily and spiritual qualities; and strives by his knowledge and his labor, to bring the world itself under his control. He renders social life more human both in the family and the civic community, through improvement of customs and institutions. Throughout the course of time he expresses, communicates and conserves in his works, great spiritual experiences and desires, that they might be of advantage to the progress of many, even of the whole human family.

Thence it follows that human culture has necessarily a historical and social aspect and the word "culture" also often assumes a sociological and ethnological sense. According to this sense we speak of a plurality of cultures. Different styles of life and multiple scales of values arise from the diverse manner of using things, of laboring, of expressing oneself, of practicing religion, of forming customs, of establishing laws and juridical institutions, of cultivating the sciences, the arts and beauty. Thus the customs handed down to it form the patrimony proper to each human community. It is also in this way that there is formed the definite, historical milieu which enfolds the man of every nation and age and from which he draws the values which permit him to promote civilization.

Section 1: The circumstances of culture in the world today.

54.   The circumstances of the life of modern man have been so profoundly changed in their social and cultural aspect, that we can speak of a new age of human history.[1] New ways are open, therefore, for the perfection and the further extension of culture. These ways have been prepared by the enormous growth of natural, human and social sciences, by technical progress, and advances in developing and organizing means whereby men can communicate with one another. Hence the culture of today possesses particular characteristics: sciences which are called exact greatly develop critical judgment; the more recent psychological studies more profoundly explain human activity; historical studies make it much easier to see things in their mutable and evolutionary aspects; customs and usages are becoming more and more uniform; industrialization, urbanization, and other causes which promote community living create a mass-culture from which are born new ways of thinking, acting and making use of leisure. The increase of commerce between the various nations and groups of men opens more widely to all the treasures of different civilizations and thus, little by little, there develops a more universal form of human culture, which better promotes and expresses the unity of the human race to the degree that it preserves the particular aspects of the different civilizations.

55.   From day to day, in every group or nation, there is an increase in the number of men and women who are conscious that they themselves are the authors and the artisans of the culture of their community. Throughout the whole world there is a mounting increase in the sense of autonomy as well as of responsibility. This is of paramount importance for the spiritual and moral maturity of the human race. This becomes more clear if we consider the unification of the world and the duty which is imposed upon us, that we build a better world based upon truth and justice. Thus we are witnesses of the birth of a new humanism, one in which

man is defined first of all by this responsibility to his brothers and to history.

56. In these conditions, it is no cause of wonder that man, who senses his responsibility for the progress of culture, nourishes a high hope but also looks with anxiety upon many contradictory things which he must resolve:

What is to be done to prevent the increased exchanges between cultures, which should lead to a true and fruitful dialogue between groups and nations, from disturbing the life of communities, from destroying the wisdom received from ancestors, or from placing in danger the character proper to each people?

How is the dynamism and expansion of a new culture to be fostered without losing a living fidelity to the heritage of tradition? This question is of particular urgency when a culture which arises from the enormous progress of science and technology must be harmonized with a culture nourished by classical studies according to various traditions.

How can we quickly and progressively harmonize the proliferation of particular branches of study with the necessity of forming a synthesis of them, and of preserving among men the faculties of contemplation and observation which lead to wisdom?

What can be done to make all men partakers of cultural values in the world, when the human culture of those who are more competent is constantly becoming more refined and more complex?

Finally how is the autonomy which culture claims for itself to be recognized as legitimate without generating a notion of humanism which is merely terrestrial, and even contrary to religion itself?

In the midst of these conflicting requirements, human culture must evolve today in such a way that it can both develop the whole human person and aid man in those duties to whose fulfilment all are called, especially Christians fraternally united in one human family.

57. Christians, on pilgrimage toward the heavenly city, should seek and think of those things which are above.[2] This duty in no way decreases, rather it increases, the importance of their obligation to work with all men in the building of a more human world. Indeed, the mystery of the Christian faith furnishes them with an excellent stimulus and aid to fulfill this duty more courageously and especially to uncover the full meaning of this activity, one which gives to human culture its eminent place in the integral vocation of man.

When man develops the earth by the work of his hands or with the aid of technology, in order that it might bear fruit and become a dwelling worthy of the whole human family and when he consciously takes part in the life of social groups, he carries out the design of God manifested at the beginning of time, that he should subdue[3] the earth, perfect creation and develop himself. At the same time he obeys the commandment of Christ that he place himself at the service of his brethren.

Furthermore, when man gives himself to the various disciplines of philosophy, history and of mathematical and natural science, and when he cultivates the arts, he can do very much to elevate the human family to a more sublime understanding of truth, goodness, and beauty, and to the formation of considered opinions which have universal value. Thus mankind may be more clearly enlightened by that marvelous Wisdom which was with God from all eternity, composing all things with Him, rejoicing in the earth, delighting in the sons of men.[4]

In this way, the human spirit, being less subjected to material things, can be more easily drawn to the worship and contemplation of the Creator. Moreover, by the impulse of grace, he is disposed to acknowledge the Word of God, Who before He became flesh in order to save all and to sum up all in Himself was already "in the world" as "the true light which enlightens every man" (John 1:9-10).[5]

Indeed today's progress in science and technology can foster a certain exclusive emphasis on observable data, and an agnosticism about everything else. For the methods of investigation which these sciences use can be wrongly considered as the supreme rule of seeking the whole truth. By virtue of their methods these sciences cannot penetrate to the intimate notion of things. Indeed the danger is present that man, confiding too much in the discoveries of today, may think that he is sufficient unto himself and no longer seek the higher things.

These unfortunate results, however, do not necessarily follow from the culture of today, nor should they lead us into the temptation of not acknowledging its positive values. Among these values are included: scientific study and fidelity toward truth in scientific enquiries, the necessity of working together with others in technical groups, a sense of international solidarity, a clearer awareness of the responsibility of experts to aid and even to protect men, the desire to make the conditions of life more favorable for all, especially for those who are poor in culture or who are deprived of the opportunity to exercise responsibility. All of these provide some preparation for the acceptance of the message of the Gospel —a preparation which can be animated by divine charity through Him Who has come to save the world.

58. There are many ties between the message of salvation and human culture. For God, revealing Himself to His people to the extent of a full manifestation of Himself in His Incarnate Son, has spoken according to the culture proper to each epoch.

Likewise the Church, living in various circumstances in the course of time, has used the discoveries of different cultures so that in her preaching she might spread and explain the message of Christ to all nations, that she might examine it and more deeply understand it, that she might give it better expression in liturgical celebration and in the varied life of the community of the faithful.

But at the same time, the Church, sent to all peoples of every time and place, is not bound exclusively and indissolubly to any race or nation, any particular way of life or any customary pattern of life recent or ancient. Faithful to her own tradition and at the same time conscious of her universal mission, she can enter into communion with the various civilizations, to their enrichment and the enrichment of the Church herself.

The Gospel of Christ constantly renews the life and culture of fallen man; it combats and removes the errors and evils resulting from the permanent allurement of sin. It never ceases to purify and elevate the morality of peoples. By riches coming from above, it makes fruitful, as it were from within, the spiritual qualities and traditions of every people and of every age. It strengthens, perfects and restores[6] them in Christ. Thus the Church, in the very fulfillment of her own function[7] stimulates and advances human and civic culture; by her action, also by her liturgy, she leads men toward interior liberty.

59. For the above reasons, the Church recalls to the mind of all that culture is to be subordinated to the integral perfection of the human person, to the good of the community and of the whole society. Therefore it is necessary to develop the human faculties in such a way that there results a growth of the faculty of wonder, of intuition, of contemplation, of making personal judgment, of developing a religious, moral and social sense.

Culture, because it flows immediately from the spiritual and social character of man, has constant need of a just freedom in order to develop; it needs also the legitimate possibility of exercising its autonomy according to its own principles. It therefore rightly demands respect and enjoys a certain inviolability within the limits of the common good, as long, of course, as it preserves the rights of the individual and the community, whether particular or universal.

This Sacred Synod, therefore, recalling the teaching of the first Vatican Council, declares that there are "two orders of knowledge" which are distinct, namely faith and reason; and that the Church does not forbid that "the human arts and disciplines use their own principles and their proper method, each in its own domain"; therefore "acknowledging this just liberty," this Sacred Synod affirms the legitimate autonomy of human culture and especially of the sciences.[8]

All this supposes that, within the limits of morality and the common utility, man can freely search for the truth, express his opinion and publish it; that he can practice any art he chooses; that finally, he can avail himself of accurate information concerning events of a public nature.[9]

As for public authority, it is not its function to determine the character of the civilization, but rather to establish the conditions and to use the means which are capable of fostering the life of culture among all even within the minorities of a nation.[10] It is necessary to do everything possible to prevent culture from being turned away from its proper end and made to serve as an instrument of political or economic power.

Section 3: Some More Urgent Duties of Christians in Regard to Culture

60. It is now possible to free most of humanity from the misery of ignorance. Therefore the duty most consonant with our times, especially for Christians, is that of working diligently for fundamental decisions to be taken in economic and political affairs, both on the national and international level, which will everywhere recognize and satisfy the right of all to a human and social culture in conformity with the dignity of the human person without any discrimination based on race, sex, nation, religion or social condition. Therefore it is necessary to provide all with a sufficient quantity of cultural benefits, especially of those which constitute the so-called basic culture lest very many be prevented from cooperating in the promotion of the common good in a truly human manner because of illiteracy and a lack of responsible activity.

We must strive to provide for those men who are gifted the possibility of pursuing higher studies; and in such a way that, as far as possible, they may occupy in society those duties, offices and services which are in harmony with their natural aptitude and the competence they have acquired.[11] Thus each man and the social groups of every people will be able to attain the full development of their culture in conformity with their qualities and traditions.

Everything must be done to make everyone conscious of the right to culture and the duty he has of developing himself culturally and of helping others. Sometimes there exist conditions of life and of work which impede the cultural striving of men and destroy in them the eagerness for culture. This is especially true of farmers and workers. It is necessary to provide for them those working conditions which will not impede their human culture but rather favor it. Women now engage in almost all spheres of activity. It is fitting that they are able to assume their proper role in accordance with their own nature. It is incumbent upon all to acknowledge and favor the proper and necessary participation of women in cultural life.

61. Today it is more difficult to form a synthesis of the various disciplines of knowledge and the arts than it was formerly. For while the mass and the diversity of cultural factors are increasing, there is a decrease in each man's faculty of perceiving and unifying these things, so that the image of "universal man" is being lost sight of more and more. Nevertheless it remains each man's duty to preserve an understanding of the whole human person in which the values of intellect, will, conscience and fraternity are pre-eminent. These values are all rooted in God the Creator and have been wonderfully restored and elevated in Christ.

The family is, as it were, the primary mother and nurse of this education. There, the children, in an atmosphere of love, more easily learn the correct order of things, while proper forms of human culture impress themselves in an almost unconscious manner upon the mind of the developing adolescent.

Opportunities for the same education are to be found also in the societies of today, due especially to the increased circulation of books and to the new means of cultural and social communication which can foster a universal culture. With the more or less universal reduction of working hours, the leisure time of most men has increased. May this leisure be used properly to relax, to fortify the health of soul and body through spontaneous study and activity, through tourism which refines man's character and enriches him with understanding of others, through sports activity which helps to preserve an equilibrium of spirit even in the community, and to establish fraternal relations among men of all conditions, nations and races. Let Christians cooperate so that the cultural manifestations and collective activity characteristic of our time may be imbued with a human and a Christian spirit.

All these leisure activities however cannot bring man to a full cultural development unless there is at the same time a profound inquiry into the meaning of culture and science for the human person.

62.   Although the Church has contributed much to the development of culture, experience shows that, because of circumstances, it is sometimes difficult to harmonize culture with Christian teaching. These difficulties do not necessarily harm the life of faith, rather they can stimulate the mind to a deeper and more accurate understanding of the faith. The recent studies and findings of science, history and philosophy raise new questions which affect life and which demand new theological investigations. Furthermore, theologians, observing the requirements and methods proper to theology, are invited to seek continually for more suitable ways of communicating doctrine to the men of their times; for the deposit of Faith or the truths are one thing and the manner in which they are enunciated, in the same meaning and understanding, is another.[12] In pastoral care, sufficient use must be made not only of theological principles, but also of the findings of the secular sciences, especially of psychology and sociology, so that the faithful may be brought to a more adequate and mature life of faith.

Literature and the arts are also, in their own way, of great importance to the life of the Church. They strive to make known the proper nature of man, his problems and his experiences in trying to know and perfect both himself and the world. They have much to do with revealing man's place in history and in the world; with illustrating the miseries and joys, the needs and strengths of man and with foreshadowing a better life for him. Thus they are able to elevate human life, expressed in manifold forms in various times and places.

Efforts must be made so that those who foster these arts feel that the Church recognizes their activity and so that, enjoying orderly freedom, they may initiate more friendly relations with the Christian community. The Church acknowledges also new forms of art which are adapted to our age and are in keeping with the characteristics of various nations and regions. They may be brought into the sanctuary since they raise the mind to God, once the manner of expression is adapted and they are conformed to liturgical requirements.[13]

Thus the knowledge of God is better manifested and the preaching of the Gospel becomes clearer to human intelligence and shows itself to be relevant to man's actual conditions of life.

May the faithful, therefore, live in very close union with the other men of their time and may they strive to understand perfectly their way of thinking and judging, as expressed in their culture. Let them blend new sciences and theories and the understanding of the most recent discoveries with Christian morality and the teaching of Christian doctrine, so that their religious culture and morality may keep pace with their scientific knowledge and with the constantly progressing technology. Thus they will be able to interpret and evaluate all things in a truly Christian spirit.

Let those who teach theology in seminaries and universities strive to collaborate with men versed in the other sciences through a sharing of their resources and points of view. Theological inquiry should pursue a profound understanding of revealed truth; at the same time it should not neglect close contact with its own time that it may be able to help those men skilled in various disciplines to attain to a better understanding of the faith. This common effort will greatly aid the formation of priests, who will be able to present to our contemporaries the doctrine of the Church concerning God, man and the world, in a manner more adapted to them so that they may receive it more willingly.[14] Furthermore, it is to be hoped that many of the laity will receive a sufficient formation in the sacred sciences and that some will dedicate themselves professionally to these studies, developing and deepening them by their own labors. In order that they may fulfill their function, let it be recognized that all the faithful, whether clerics or laity, possess a lawful freedom of inquiry, freedom of thought and of expressing their mind with humility and fortitude in those matters on which they enjoy competence.[15]

CHAPTER III

ECONOMIC AND SOCIAL LIFE

63.   In the economic and social realms, too, the dignity and complete vocation of the human person and the welfare of society as a whole are to be respected and promoted. For man is the source, the center, and the purpose of all economic and social life.

Like other areas of social life, the economy of today is marked by man's increasing domination over nature, by closer and more intense relationships between citizens, groups, and countries and their mutual dependence, and by the increased intervention of the state. At the same time progress in the methods of production and in the exchange of goods and services has made the economy an instrument capable of better meeting the intensified needs of the human family.

Reasons for anxiety, however, are not lacking. Many people, especially in economically advanced areas, seem, as it were, to be ruled by economics, so that almost their entire personal and social life is permeated with a certain economic way of thinking. Such is true both of nations that favor a collective economy and of others. At the very time when the development of economic life could mitigate social inequalities (provided that it be guided and coordinated in a reasonable and human way), it is often made to embitter them; or, in some places, it even results in a decline of the social status of the underprivileged and in contempt for the poor. While an immense number of people still lack the absolute necessities of life, some, even in less advanced areas, live in luxury or squander wealth. Extravagance and wretchedness exist side by side. While a few enjoy very great power of choice, the majority are deprived of almost all possibility of acting on their own initiative and responsibility, and often subsist in living and working conditions unworthy of the human person.

A similar lack of economic and social balance is to be noticed between agriculture, industry, and the services, and also between different parts of one and the same country. The contrast between the economically more advanced countries and other countries is becoming more serious day by day, and the very peace of the world can be jeopardized thereby.

Our contemporaries are coming to feel these inequalities with an ever sharper awareness, since they are thoroughly convinced that the ampler technical and economic possibilities which the world of today enjoys can and should correct this unhappy state of affairs. Hence, many reforms in the socio-economic realm and a change of mentality and attitude are required of all. For this reason the Church down through the centuries and in the light of the Gospel has worked out the principles of justice and equity demanded by right reason both for individual and social life and for international life, and she has proclaimed them especially in recent times. This Sacred Council intends to strengthen these principles according to the circumstances of this age and to set forth certain guidelines, especially with regard to the requirements of economic development.[1]

Section 1. Economic Development

64. Today more than ever before attention is rightly given to the increase of the production of agricultural and industrial goods and of the rendering of services, for the purpose of making provision for the growth of population and of satisfying the increasing desires of the human race. Therefore, technical progress, an inventive spirit, an eagerness to create and to expand enterprises, the application of methods of production, and the strenuous efforts of all who engage in production—in a word, all the elements making for such development—must be promoted. The fundamental purpose of this production is not the mere increase of products nor profit or control but rather the service of man, and indeed of the whole man with regard for the full range of his material needs and

the demands of his intellectual, moral, spiritual, and religious life; this applies to every man whatsoever and to every group of men, of every race and of every part of the world. Consequently, economic activity is to be carried on according to its own methods and laws within the limits of the moral order,[2] so that God's plan for mankind may be realized.[3]

65. Economic development must remain under man's determination and must not be left to the judgment of a few men or groups possessing too much economic power or of the political community alone or of certain more powerful nations. It is necessary, on the contrary, that at every level the largest possible number of people and, when it is a question of international relations, all nations have an active share in directing that development. There is need as well of the coordination and fitting and harmonious combination of the spontaneous efforts of individuals and of free groups with the undertakings of public authorities.

Growth is not to be left solely to a kind of mechanical course of economic activity of individuals, nor to the authority of government. For this reason, doctrines which obstruct the necessary reforms under the guise of a false liberty, and those which subordinate the basic rights of individual persons and groups to the collective organization of production must be shown to be erroneous.[4]

Citizens, on the other hand, should remember that it is their right and duty, which is also to be recognized by the civil authority, to contribute to the true progress of their own community according to their ability. Especially in underdeveloped areas, where all resources must urgently be employed, those who hold back their unproductive resources or who deprive their community of the material or spiritual aid that it needs—saving the personal right of migration—gravely endanger the common good.

66. To satisfy the demands of justice and equity, strenuous efforts must be made, without disregarding the rights of persons or the natural qualities of each country, to remove as quickly as possible the immense economic inequalities, which now exist and in many cases are growing and which are connected with individual

and social discrimination. Likewise, in many areas, in view of the special difficulties of agriculture relative to the raising and selling of produce, country people must be helped both to increase and to market what they produce, and to introduce the necessary development and renewal and also obtain a fair income. Otherwise, as too often happens, they will remain in the condition of lower-class citizens. Let farmers themselves, especially young ones, apply themselves to perfecting their professional skill, for without it, there can be no agricultural advance.[5]

Justice and equity likewise require that the mobility, which is necessary in a developing economy, be regulated in such a way as to keep the life of individuals and their families from becoming insecure and precarious. When workers come from another country or district and contribute to the economic advancement of a nation or region by their labor, all discrimination as regards wages and working conditions must be carefully avoided. All the people, moreover, above all the public authorities, must treat them not as mere tools of production but as persons, and must help them to bring their families to live with them and to provide themselves with a decent dwelling; they must also see to it that these workers are incorporated into the social life of the country or region that receives them. Employment opportunities, however, should be created in their own areas as far as possible.

In economic affairs which today are subject to change, as in the new forms of industrial society in which automation, for example, is advancing, care must be taken that sufficient and suitable work and the possibility of the appropriate technical and professional formation are furnished. The livelihood and the human dignity especially of those who are in very difficult conditions because of illness or old age must be guaranteed.

Section 2. Certain Principles Governing Socio-Economic Life as a Whole

67. Human labor which is expended in the production and exchange of goods or in the performance of economic services is

superior to the other elements of economic life, for the latter have only the nature of tools.

This labor, whether it is engaged in independently or hired by someone else, comes immediately from the person, who as it were stamps the things of nature with his seal and subdues them to his will. By his labor a man ordinarily supports himself and his family, is joined to his fellow men and serves them, and can exercise genuine charity and be a partner in the work of bringing divine creation to perfection. Indeed, we hold that through labor offered to God man is associated with the redemptive work of Jesus Christ, Who conferred an eminent dignity on labor when at Nazareth He worked with His own hands. From this there follows for every man the duty of working faithfully and also the right to work. It is the duty of society, moreover, according to the circumstances prevailing in it, and in keeping with its role, to help the citizens to find sufficient employment. Finally, remuneration for labor is to be such that man may be furnished the means to cultivate worthily his own material, social, cultural, and spiritual life and that of his dependents, in view of the function and productiveness of each one, the conditions of the factory or workshop, and the common good.[6]

Since economic activity for the most part implies the associated work of human beings, any way of organizing and directing it which might be detrimental to any working men and women would be wrong and inhuman. It happens too often, however, even in our days, that workers are reduced to the level of being slaves to their own work. This is by no means justified by the so-called economic laws. The entire process of productive work, therefore, must be adapted to the needs of the person and to his way of life, above all to his domestic life, especially in respect to mothers of families, always with due regard for sex and age. The opportunity, moreover, should be granted to workers to unfold their own abilities and personality through the performance of their work. Applying their time and strength to their employment with a due sense of responsibility, they should also all enjoy sufficient rest and leisure to cultivate their familial, cultural, social and religious life. They

71

should also have the opportunity freely to develop the energies and potentialities which perhaps they cannot bring to much fruition in their professional work.

68.   In economic enterprises it is persons who are joined together, that is, free and independent human beings created to the image of God. Therefore, taking account of the prerogatives of each —owners or employers, management or labor—and without doing harm to the necessary unity of management, the active sharing of all in the administration and profits of these enterprises in ways to be properly determined should be promoted.[7] Since more often, however, decisions concerning economic and social conditions, on which the future lot of the workers and of their children depends, are made not within the the business itself but by institutions on a higher level, the workers themselves should have a share also in determining these conditions—in person or through freely elected delegates.

Among the basic rights of the human person is to be numbered the right of freely founding unions for working people. These should be able truly to represent them and to contribute to the organizing of economic life in the right way. Included is the right of freely taking part in the activity of these unions without risk of reprisal. Through this orderly participation joined to progressive economic and social formation, all will grow day by day in the awareness of their own function and responsibility, and thus they will be brought to feel that they are comrades in the whole task of economic development and in the attainment of the universal common good according to their capacities and aptitudes.

When, however, socio-economic disputes arise, efforts must be made to come to a peaceful settlement. Although recourse must always be had first to a sincere dialogue between the parties, the strike, nevertheless, can remain even in present-day circumstances a necessary, though ultimate, means for the defense of the workers' own rights and the fulfillment of their just desires. As soon as possible, however, ways should be sought to resume negotiations and discussions leading toward reconciliation.

69. God intended the earth with everything contained in it for the use of all human beings and peoples. Thus, under the guidance of justice together with charity, created goods should be in abundance for all in an equitable manner.[8] Whatever the forms of property may be, as adapted to the legitimate institutions of peoples, according to diverse and changeable circumstances, attention must always be paid to this universal goal of earthly goods. In using them, therefore, man should regard the external things that he legitimately possesses not only as his own but also as common in the sense that they should be able to benefit not only him but also others as well.[9] On the other hand, the right of having a share of earthly goods sufficient for oneself and one's family belongs to everyone. The Fathers and Doctors of the Church held this opinion, teaching that men are obliged to come to the relief of the poor and to do so not merely out of their superfluous goods.[10] If one is in extreme necessity, he has the right to procure for himself what he needs out of the riches of others.[11] Since there are so many people prostrate with hunger in the world, this Sacred Council urges all, both individuals and governments, to remember the aphorism of the Fathers, "Feed the man dying of hunger, because if you have not fed him, you have killed him,"[12] and really to share and use their earthly goods, according to the ability of each, especially by supporting individuals or peoples with the aid by which they may be able to help and develop themselves.

In economically less advanced societies the common destination of earthly goods is partly satisfied by means of the customs and traditions proper to the community, by which the absolute essentials are furnished to each member. An effort must be made, however, to avoid regarding certain customs as altogether unchangeable, if they no longer answer the new needs of this age. On the other hand, imprudent action should not be taken against respectable customs which, provided they are suitably adapted to present-day circumstances, do not cease to be very useful. Similarly in highly developed nations a body of social institutions dealing with protection and security can, for its own part, bring to reality the common destination of earthly goods. Family and social services, especially those that provide for culture and education, should be further promoted. When all these things are being organized, vigilance is necessary to prevent the citizens from being led into a certain inertia vis-a-vis society or from rejecting the burden of taking up office or from refusing to serve.

70. Investments, for their part, must be directed toward providing employment and sufficient income for the people both now and in the future. Whoever make decisions concerning these investments and the planning of the economy—whether they be individuals or groups or public authorities—are bound to keep these objectives in mind and to recognize their serious obligation of making sure, on the one hand, that provision be made for the necessities required for a decent life both of individuals and of the whole community and, on the other, of looking out for the future and of establishing a proper balance between the needs of present-day consumption, both individual and collective, and the demands of investing for the generation to come. They should also always bear in mind the urgent needs of underdeveloped countries or regions. In monetary matters they should beware of hurting the welfare of their own country or of other countries. Care should also be taken lest the economically weak countries unjustly suffer any loss from a change in the value of money.

71. Since property and other forms of private ownership of external goods contribute to the expression of the personality, and since, moreover, they furnish one an occasion to exercise his function in society and in the economy, it is very important that the access of both individuals and communities to some ownership of external goods be fostered.

Private propery or some ownership of external goods confers on everyone a sphere wholly necessary for the autonomy of the person and the family, and it should be regarded as an extension of human freedom. Lastly, since it adds incentives for carrying on one's function and duty, it constitutes one of the conditions for civil liberties.[13]

The forms of such ownership of property are varied today and are becoming increasingly diversified. They all remain, however, a cause of security not to be underestimated, in spite of social funds, rights, and services provided by society. This is true not only of material goods but also of intangible goods such as professional skills.

The right of private ownership, however, is not opposed to the right inherent in various forms of public property. Goods can be transferred to the public domain only by the competent authority, according to the demands and within the limits of the common good, and with fair compensation. Furthermore, it is the right of public authority to prevent anyone from misusing his private property to the detriment of the common good.[14]

By its very nature private property has a social quality which is based on the law of the common destination of earthly goods.[15] If this social quality is overlooked, property often becomes an occasion of a passionate desire for wealth and serious disturbances, so that a pretext is given to those who attack private property for calling the right itself into question.

In many underdeveloped regions there are large or even extensive rural estates which are only slightly cultivated or lie completely idle for the sake of profit, while the majority of the people either are without land or have only very small fields, and, on the other hand, it is evidently urgent to increase the productivity of the fields. Not infrequently those who are hired to work for the landowners or who till a portion of the land as tenants receive a wage or income unworthy of a human being, lack decent housing and are exploited by middlemen. Deprived of all security, they live under such personal servitude that almost every opportunity of acting on their own initiative and responsibility is denied to them and all advancement in human culture and all sharing in social and political life is forbidden to them. According to different circumstances, therefore, reforms are necessary: that income may grow, working conditions should be improved, security in employment increased, and an incentive to working on one's own initiative given. Indeed, insufficiently cultivated estates should be distributed to those who can make these lands fruitful; in this case, the necessary ways and means, especially educational aids and the right facilities for cooperative organization, must be supplied. Whenever, nevertheless, the common good requires expropriation, compensation must be reckoned in equity after all the circumstances have been weighed.

72.   Christians who take an active part in present-day socio-economic development and fight for justice and charity should be convinced that they can make a great contribution to the prosperity of mankind and to the peace of the world. In these activities let them, either as individuals or as members of groups, give a shining example. Having acquired the skills and experience which are absolutely necessary, they should observe the right order in their earthly activities in faithfulness to Christ and His Gospel. Thus their whole life, both individual and social, will be permeated with the spirit of the beatitudes, notably with a spirit of poverty.

Whoever in obedience to Christ seeks first the Kingdom of God, takes therefrom a stronger and purer love for helping all his brethren and for perfecting the work of justice under the inspiration of charity.[16]

CHAPTER IV

THE LIFE OF THE POLITICAL COMMUNITY

73.   In our day, profound changes are apparent also in the structure and institutions of peoples. These result from their cultural, economic and social evolution. Such changes have a great influence on the life of the political community, especially regarding the rights and duties of all in the exercise of civil freedom and in the attainment of the common good, and in organizing the relations of citizens among themselves and with respect to public authority.

The present keener sense of human dignity has given rise in many parts of the world to attempts to bring about a politico-juridical order which will give better protection to the rights of the person in public life. These include the right freely to meet and form associations, the right to express one's own opinion and to profess one's religion both publicly and privately. The protection of the rights of a person is indeed a necessary condition so that citizens, individually or collectively, can take an active part in the life and government of the state.

Along with cultural, economic and social development, there is a growing desire among many people to play a greater part in organizing the life of the political community. In the conscience of many there arises an increasing concern that the rights of minorities be recognized, without any neglect for their duties toward the political community. In addition, there is a steadily growing respect for men of other opinions or other religions. At the same time, there is wider cooperation to guarantee the actual exercise of personal rights to all citizens, and not only to a few privileged individuals.

However, those political systems, prevailing in some parts of the world are to be reproved which hamper civic or religious freedom, victimize large numbers through avarice and political crimes, and divert the exercise of authority from the service of the common good to the interests of one or another faction or of the rulers themselves.

There is no better way to establish political life on a truly human basis than by fostering an inward sense of justice and kindliness, and of service to the common good, and by strengthening basic convictions as to the true nature of the political community and the purpose, right exercise, and sphere of action of public authority.

74.   Men, families and the various groups which make up the civil community are aware that they cannot achieve a truly human life by their own unaided efforts. They see the need for a wider community, within which each one makes his specific contribution every day toward an ever broader realization of the common good.[1] For this purpose they set up a political community which takes various forms. The political community exists, consequently, for the sake of the common good, in which it finds its full justification and significance, and the source of its inherent legitimacy. Indeed, the common good embraces the sum of those conditions of the social life whereby men, families and associations more adequately and readily may attain their own perfection.[2]

Yet the people who come together in the political community are many and diverse, and they have every right to prefer divergent solutions. If the political community is not to be torn apart while everyone follows his own opinion, there must be an authority to direct the energies of all citizens toward the common good, not in a mechanical or despotic fashion, but by acting above all as a moral force which appeals to each one's freedom and sense of responsibility.

It is clear, therefore, that the political community and public authority are founded on human nature and hence belong to the order designed by God, even though the choice of a political regime and the appointment of rulers are left to the free will of citizens.[3]

It follows also that political authority, both in the community as such and in the representative bodies of the state, must always be exercised within the limits of the moral order and directed toward the common good—with a dynamic concept of that good—according to the juridical order legitimately established or which should be established. When authority is so exercised, citizens are bound in conscience to obey.[4] Accordingly, the responsibility, dignity and importance of leaders are indeed clear.

But where citizens are oppressed by a public authority overstepping its competence, they should not protest against those things which are objectively required for the common good; but it is legitimate for them to defend their own rights and the rights of their fellow citizens against the abuse of this authority, while keeping within those limits drawn by the natural law and the Gospels.

According to the character of different peoples and their historic development, the political community can, however, adopt a variety of concrete solutions in its structures and the organization of public authority. For the benefit of the whole human family, these solutions must always contribute to the formation of a type of man who will be cultivated, peace-loving and well-disposed towards all his fellow men.

75. It is in full conformity with human nature that there should be juridico-political structures providing all citizens in an ever better fashion and without any discrimination the practical possibility of freely and actively taking part in the establishment of the juridical foundations of the political community and in the direction of public affairs, in fixing the terms of reference of the various public bodies and in the election of political leaders.[5] All citizens, therefore, should be mindful of the right and also the duty to use

their free vote to further the common good. The Church praises and esteems the work of those who for the good of men devote themselves to the service of the state and take on the burdens of this office.

If the citizens' responsible cooperation is to produce the good results which may be expected in the normal course of political life, there must be a statute of positive law providing for a suitable division of the functions and bodies of authority and an efficient and independent system for the protection of rights. The rights of all persons, families and groups, and their practical application, must be recognized, respected and furthered, together with the duties binding on all citizens.[6] Among the latter, it will be well to recall the duty of rendering the political community such material and personal services as are required by the common good. Rulers must be careful not to hamper the development of family, social or cultural groups, nor that of intermediate bodies or organizations, and not to deprive them of opportunities for legitimate and constructive activity; they should willingly seek rather to promote the orderly pursuit of such activity. Citizens, for their part, either individually or collectively, must be careful not to attribute excessive power to public authority, not to make exaggerated and untimely demands upon it in their own interests, lessening in this way the responsible role of persons, families and social groups.

The complex circumstances of our day make it necessary for public authority to intervene more often in social, economic and cultural matters in order to bring about favorable conditions which will give more effective help to citizens and groups in their free pursuit of man's total well-being. The relations, however, between socialization[7] and the autonomy and development of the person can be understood in different ways according to various regions and the evolution of peoples. But when the exercise of rights is restricted temporarily for the common good, freedom should be restored immediately upon change of circumstances. Moreover, it is inhuman for public authority to fall back on dictatorial systems or totalitarian methods which violate the rights of the person or social groups.

80

Citizens must cultivate a generous and loyal spirit of patriotism, but without being narrow-minded. This means that they will always direct their attention to the good of the whole human family, united by the different ties which bind together races, people and nations.

All Christians must be aware of their own specific vocation within the political community. It is for them to give an example by their sense of responsibility and their service of the common good. In this way they are to demonstrate concretely how authority can be compatible with freedom, personal initiative with the solidarity of the whole social organism, and the advantages of unity with fruitful diversity. They must recognize the legitimacy of different opinions with regard to temporal solutions, and respect citizens, who, even as a group, defend their points of view by honest methods. Political parties, for their part, must promote those things which in their judgment are required for the common good; it is never allowable to give their interests priority over the common good.

Great care must be taken with regard to civic and political formation, which is of the utmost necessity today for the population as a whole, and especially for youth, so that all citizens can play their part in the life of the political community. Those who are suited or can become suited should prepare themselves for the difficult, but at the same time, the very noble art of politics,[8] and should seek to practice this art without regard for their own interests or for material advantages. With integrity and wisdom, they must take action against any form of injustice and tyranny, against arbitrary domination by an individual or a political party, and any intolerance. They should dedicate themselves to the service of all with sincerity and fairness, indeed, with the charity and fortitude demanded by political life.

76. It is very important, especially where a pluralistic society prevails, that there be a correct notion of the relationship between the political community and the Church, and a clear distinction between the tasks which Christians undertake, individually

or as a group, on their own responsibility as citizens guided by the dictates of a Christian conscience, and the activities which, in union with their pastors, they carry out in the name of the Church.

The Church, by reason of her role and competence, is not identified in any way with the political community nor bound to any political system. She is at once a sign and a safeguard of the transcendent character of the human person.

The Church and the political community in their own fields are autonomous and independent from each other. Yet both, under different titles, are devoted to the personal and social vocation of the same men. The more that both foster healthier cooperation between themselves with due consideration for the circumstances of time and place, the more effective will their service be exercised for the good of all. For man's horizons are not limited only to the temporal order: while living in the context of human history, he preserves intact his eternal vocation. The Church, for her part, founded on the love of the Redeemer, contributes toward the reign of justice and charity within the borders of a nation and between nations. By preaching the truths of the Gospel, and bringing to bear on all fields of human endeavor the light of her doctrine and of a Christian witness, she respects and fosters the political freedom and responsibility of citizens.

The Apostles, their successors and those who cooperate with them, are sent to announce to mankind Christ, the Saviour. Their apostolate is based on the power of God, Who very often shows forth the strength of the Gospel in the weaknes of its witnesses. All those dedicated to the ministry of God's Word must use the ways and means proper to the Gospel which in a great many respects differ from the means proper to the earthly city.

There are, indeed, close links between earthly things and those elements of man's condition which transcend the world. The Church herself makes use of temporal things insofar as her own mission requires it. She, for her part, does not place her trust in the privileges offered by civil authority. She will even give up the exercise of certain rights which have been legitimately acquired, if it becomes clear that their use will cast doubt on the sincerity of her witness or that new ways of life demand new methods. It is only right, however, that at all times and in all places, the Church should have true freedom to preach the faith, to teach her social doctrine, to exercise her role freely among men, and also to pass moral judgment in those matters which concern public order when the fundamental rights of a person or the salvation of souls require it. In this, she should make use of all the means—but only those —which accord with the Gospel and which correspond to the general good with due regard to the diverse circumstances of time and place.

While faithfully adhering to the Gospel and fulfilling her mission to the world, the Church, whose duty it is to foster and elevate [9] all that is found to be true, good and beautiful in the human community, strengthens peace among men for the glory of God.[10]

CHAPTER V

THE FOSTERING OF PEACE AND THE PROMOTION OF A COMMUNITY OF NATIONS

77. In our generation when men continue to be afflicted by acute hardships and anxieties arising from the ravages of war or the threat of it, the whole human family faces an hour of supreme crisis in its advance toward maturity. Moving gradually together and everywhere more conscious already of its unity, this family cannot accomplish its task of constructing for all men everywhere a world more genuinely human unless each person devotes himself to the cause of peace with renewed vigor. Thus it happens that the Gospel message, which is in harmony with the loftier strivings and aspirations of the human race, takes on a new luster in our day as it declares that the artisans of peace are blessed "because they will be called the sons of God" (Matt. 5:9).

Consequently, as it points out the authentic and noble meaning of peace and condemns the frightfulness of war, the Council wishes passionately to summon Christians to cooperate, under the help of Christ, the author of peace, with all men in securing among themselves a peace based on justice and love and in setting up the instruments of peace.

78. Peace is not merely the absence of war; nor can it be reduced solely to the maintenance of a balance of power between enemies; nor is it brought about by dictatorship. Instead, it is rightly and appropriately called an enterprise of justice (Is. 32:7). Peace results from that order structured into human society by its

divine Founder, and actualized by men as they thirst after ever greater justice. The common good of humanity finds its ultimate meaning in the eternal law. But since the concrete demands of this common good are constantly changing as time goes on, peace is never attained once and for all, but must be built up ceaselessly. Moreover, since the human will is unsteady and wounded by sin, the achievement of peace requires a constant mastering of passions and the vigilance of lawful authority.

But this is not enough. This peace on earth cannot be obtained unless personal well-being is safeguarded and men freely and trustingly share with one another the riches of their inner spirits and their talents. A firm determination to respect other men and peoples and their dignity, as well as the studied practice of brotherhood are absolutely necessary for the establishment of peace. Hence peace is likewise the fruit of love, which goes beyond what justice can provide.

That earthly peace which arises from love of neighbor symbolizes and results from the peace of Christ which radiates from God the Father. For by the Cross the Incarnate Son, the Prince of Peace reconciled all men with God. By thus restoring all men to the unity of one people and one body, He slew hatred in His own flesh;[1] and, after being lifted on high by His resurrection, He poured forth the spirit of love into the hearts of men.

For this reason, all Christians are urgently summoned to do in love what the truth requires (Eph. 4:15), and to join with all true peacemakers in pleading for peace and bringing it about.

Motivated by this same spirit, we cannot fail to praise those who renounce the use of violence in the vindication of their rights and who resort to methods of defense which are otherwise available to weaker parties too, provided this can be done without injury to the rights and duties of others or of the community itself.

Insofar as men are sinful, the threat of war hangs over them, and hang over them it will until the return of Christ. But insofar as men vanquish sin by a union of love, they will vanquish violence

85

as well and make these words come true: "They shall turn their swords into plough-shares, and their spears into sickles. Nation shall not lift up sword against nation, neither shall they learn war any more" (Isaias 2:4).

Section I: The Avoidance of War

79. In spite of the fact that recent wars have wrought physical and moral havoc on our world, war produces its devastation day by day in some part of the world. Indeed, now that every kind of weapon produced by modern science is used in war, the fierce character of warfare threatens to lead the combatants to a savagery far surpassing that of the past. Furthermore, the complexity of the modern world and the intricacy of international relations allow guerrilla warfare to be carried on by new methods of deceit and subversion. In many cases the use of terrorism is regarded as a new way to wage war.

Contemplating this melancholy state of humanity, the Council wishes, above all things else, to recall the permanent binding force of universal natural law and its all-embracing principles. Man's conscience itself gives ever more emphatic voice to these principles. Therefore, actions which deliberately conflict with these same principles, as well as orders commanding such actions are criminal, and blind obedience cannot excuse those who yield to them. The most infamous among these are actions designed for the methodical extermination of an entire people, nation or ethnic minority. Such actions must be vehemently condemned as horrendous crimes. The courage of those who fearlessly and openly resist those who issue such commands merits the highest commendation.

On the subject of war, quite a large number of nations have subscribed to international agreements aimed at making military activity and its consequences less inhuman. Their stipulations deal with such matters as the treatment of wounded soldiers and prisoners. Agreements of this sort must be honored. Indeed they should be improved upon so that the frightfulness of war can be better and more workably held in check. All men, especially government officials and experts in these matters, are bound to do everything they can to effect these improvements. Moreover, it seems right that laws make humane provisions for the case of those who for reasons of conscience refuse to bear arms, provided however, that they agree to serve the human community in some other way.

Certainly, war has not been rooted out of human affairs. As long as the danger of war remains and there is no competent and sufficiently powerful authority at the international level, governments cannot be denied the right to legitimate defense once every means of peaceful settlement has been exhausted. Government authorities and others who share public responsibility have the duty to conduct such grave matters soberly and to protect the welfare of the people entrusted to their care. But it is one thing to undertake military action for the just defense of the people, and something else again to seek the subjugation of other nations. Nor, by the same token, does the mere fact that war has unhappily begun mean that all is fair between the warring parties.

Those too who devote themselves to the military service of their country should regard themselves as the agents of security and freedom of peoples. As long as they fulfill this role properly, they are making a genuine contribution to the establishment of peace.

80. The horror and perversity of war is immensely magnified by the increase in the number of scientific weapons. For acts of war involving these weapons can inflict massive and indiscriminate destruction, thus going far beyond the bounds of legitimate defense. Indeed, if the kind of instruments which can now be found in the armories of the great nations were to be employed to their fullest, an almost total and altogether reciprocal slaughter of each side by the other would follow, not to mention the widespread devastation that would take place in the world and the deadly after effects that would be spawned by the use of weapons of this kind.

All these considerations compel us to undertake an evaluation of war with an entirely new attitude.[2] The men of our time must realize that they will have to give a somber reckoning of their deeds of war for the course of the future will depend greatly on the decisions they make today.

With these truths in mind, this most Holy Synod makes its own the condemnations of total war already pronounced by recent popes,[3] and issues the following declaration:

Any act of war aimed indiscriminately at the destruction of entire cities or extensive areas along with their population is a crime against God and man himself. It merits unequivocal and unhesitating condemnation.

The unique hazard of modern warfare consists in this: it provides those who possess modern scientific weapons with a kind of occasion for perpetrating just such abominations; moreover, through a certain inexorable chain of events, it can catapult men into the most atrocious decisions. That such may never happen in the future, the bishops of the whole world gathered together, beg all men, especially government officials and military leaders, to give unremitting thought to their tremendous responsibility before God and the entire human race.

81. Scientific weapons, to be sure, are not amassed solely for use in war. Since the defensive strength of any nation is considered to be dependent upon its capacity for immediate retaliation, this accumulation of arms, which increases each year, likewise serves, in a way heretofore unknown, as a deterrent to possible enemy attack. Many regard this as the most effective way by which peace of a sort can be maintained between nations at the present time.

Whatever be the facts about this method of deterrence, men should be convinced that the arms race in which an already considerable number of countries are engaged is not a safe way to preserve a steady peace, nor is the so-called balance resulting from this race a sure and authentic peace. Rather than being eliminated thereby, the causes of war are in danger of being gradually aggravated. While extravagant sums are being spent for the furnishing of ever new weapons, an adequate remedy cannot be provided for the multiple miseries afflicting the whole modern world. Disagreements between nations are not really and radically healed; on the contrary, they spread the infection to other parts of the earth. New approaches based on reformed attitudes must be taken to remove this trap and to emancipate the world from its crushing anxiety through the restoration of genuine peace.

Therefore, we say it again: the arms race is an utterly treacherous trap for humanity, and one which ensnares the poor to an intolerable degree. It is much to be feared that if this race persists, it will eventually spawn all the lethal ruin whose path it is now making ready. Warned by the calamities which the human race has made possible, let us make use of the interlude granted us from above and for which we are thankful, to become more conscious of our own responsibility and to find means for resolving our disputes in a manner more worthy of man. Divine Providence urgently demands of us that we free ourselves from the age-old slavery of war. If we refuse to make this effort, we do not know where we will be led by the evil road we have set upon.

82.   It is our clear duty, therefore, to strain every muscle in working for the time when all war can be completely outlawed by international consent. This goal undoubtedly requires the establishment of some universal public authority acknowledged as such by all and endowed with the power to safeguard on the behalf of all, security, regard for justice, and respect for rights. But before this hoped for authority can be set up, the highest existing international centers must devote themselves vigorously to the pursuit of better means for obtaining common security. Since peace must be born of mutual trust between nations and not be imposed on them through fear of the available weapons, everyone must labor to put an end at last to the arms race, and to make a true beginning of disarmament, not unilaterally indeed, but proceeding at an equal pace according to agreement, and backed up by adequate and workable safeguards.[4]

In the meantime, efforts which have already been made and are still under way to eliminate the danger of war are not to be underrated. On the contrary, support should be given to the good will of the very many leaders who work hard to do away with war, which they abominate. These men, although burdened by the extremely weighty preoccupations of their high office, are nonetheless moved by the very grave peacemaking task to which they are bound, even if they cannot ignore the complexity of matters as they stand. We should fervently ask God to give these men the strength to go forward perseveringly and to follow through courageously on this work of building peace with vigor. It is a work of supreme love for mankind. Today it certainly demands that they extend their thoughts and their spirit beyond the confines of their own nation, that they put aside national selfishness and ambition to dominate other nations, and that they nourish a profound reverence for the whole of humanity, which is already making its way so laboriously toward greater unity.

The problems of peace and of disarmament have already been the subject of extensive, strenuous and constant examination. Together with international meetings dealing with these problems, such studies should be regarded as the first steps toward solving these serious questions, and should be promoted with even greater urgency by way of yielding concrete results in the future.

Nevertheless, men should take heed not to entrust themselves only to the efforts of others, while not caring about their own attitudes. For government officials who must at one and the same time guarantee the good of their own people and promote the universal good are very greatly dependent on public opinion and feeling. It does them no good to work for peace as long as feelings of hostility, contempt and distrust, as well as racial hatred and unbending ideologies, continue to divide men and place them in opposing camps. Consequently there is above all a pressing need for a renewed education of attitudes and for new inspiration in public opinion. Those who are dedicated to the work of education, particularly of the young, or who mold public opinion, should consider it their most weighty task to instruct all in fresh sentiments of peace. Indeed, we all need a change of heart as we regard the entire world and those tasks which we can perform in unison for the betterment of our race.

But we should not let false hope deceive us. For unless enmities and hatred are put away and firm, honest agreements concerning world peace are reached in the future, humanity, which already is in the middle of a grave crisis, even though it is endowed with remarkable knowledge, will perhaps be brought to that dismal hour in which it will experience no peace other than the dreadful peace of death. But, while we say this, the Church of Christ, present in the midst of the anxiety of this age, does not cease to hope most firmly. She intends to propose to our age over and over again, in season and out of season, this apostolic message: "Behold, now is the acceptable time for a change of heart; behold! now is the day of salvation." [5]

Section II: Setting Up an International Community

83.   In order to build up peace the causes of discord among men, especially injustice, which foment wars must above all be rooted out. Not a few of these causes come from excessive economic inequalities and from putting off the steps needed to remedy them. Other causes of discord, however, have their source in the desire to dominate and in a contempt for persons. And, if we look for deeper causes, we find them in human envy, distrust, pride, and other egotistical passions. Man cannot bear so many ruptures in the harmony of things. Consequently, the world is constantly beset by strife and violence between men, even when no war is being waged. Besides, since these same evils are present in the relations between various nations as well, in order to overcome or forestall them and to keep violence once unleashed within limits, it is absolutely necessary for countries to cooperate to better advantage, to work together more closely, and jointly to organize international bodies and to work tirelessly for the creation of organizations which will foster peace.

84.   In view of the increasingly close ties of mutual dependence today between all the inhabitants and peoples of the earth,

the fitting pursuit and effective realization of the universal common good now require of the community of nations that it organize itself in a manner suited to its present responsibilities, especially toward the many parts of the world which are still suffering from unbearable want.

To reach this goal, organizations of the international community, for their part, must make provision for men's different needs, both in the fields of social life—such as food supplies, health, education, labor and also in certain special circumstances which can crop up here and there, e.g., the need to promote the general improvement of developing countries, or to alleviate the distressing conditions in which refugees dispersed throughout the world find themselves, or also to assist migrants and their families.

International and regional organizations which are already in existence are certainly well-deserving of the human race. These are the first efforts at laying the foundations on an international level for a community of all men to work for the solution to the serious problems of our times, to encourage progress everywhere, and to obviate wars of whatever kind. In all of these activities the Church rejoices in the spirit of true brotherhood flourishing between Christians and non-Christians as it strives to make ever more strenuous efforts to relieve widespread misery.

85. The present solidarity of mankind also calls for a revival of greater international cooperation in the economic field. Although nearly all peoples have become autonomous, they are far from being free of every form of undue dependence, and far from escaping all danger of serious internal difficulties.

The development of a nation depends on human and financial aids. The citizens of each country must be prepared by education and professional training to discharge the various tasks of economic and social life. But this in turn requires the aid of foreign specialists who, when they give aid, will not act as overlords, but as helpers and fellow-workers. Developing nations will not be able to procure material assistance unless radical changes are made in the established procedures of modern world commerce. Other aid should be provided as well by advanced nations in the form of gifts, loans or financial investments. Such help should be accorded with generosity and without greed on the one side, and received with complete honesty on the other side.

If an authentic economic order is to be established on a worldwide basis, an end will have to be put to profiteering, to national ambition, to the appetite for political supremacy, to militaristic calculations, and to machinations for the purpose of spreading and imposing ideologies.

86. The following norms seem useful for such cooperation:

a) Developing nations should take great pains to seek as the object of progress to express and secure the total human fulfillment of their citizens. They should bear in mind that progress arises and grows above all out of the labor and genius of the nations themselves because it has to be based, not only on foreign aid, but especially on the full utilization of their own resources, and on the development of their own culture and traditions. Those who exert the greatest influence on others should be outstanding in this respect.

b) On the other hand, it is a very important duty of the advanced nations to help the developing nations in discharging their above-mentioned responsibilities. They should therefore gladly carry out on their own home front those spiritual and material readjustments that are required for the realization of this universal cooperation.

Consequently, in business dealings with weaker and poorer nations, they should be careful to respect their welfare, for these countries need the income they receive on the sale of their homemade products to support themselves.

c) It is the role of the international community to coordinate and promote development, but in such a way that the resources earmarked for this purpose will be allocated as effectively as possible, and with complete equity. It is likewise this community's duty, with due regard for the principle of subsidiarity, so to regulate economic relations throughout the world that these will be carried out in accordance with the norms of justice.

Suitable organizations should be set up to foster and regulate international business affairs, particularly with the underdeveloped countries, and to compensate for losses resulting from an excessive inequality of power among the various nations. This type of organization, in unison with technical, cultural, and financial aid, should provide the help which developing nations need so that they can advantageously pursue their own economic advancement.

d) In many cases there is an urgent need to revamp economic and social structures. But one must guard against proposed technical solutions that are untimely. This is particularly true of those solutions providing man with material conveniences, which are nevertheless contrary to man's spiritual nature and advancement. For "not by bread alone does man live, but by every word which proceeds from the mouth of God" (Matt. 4:4). Every sector of the family of man carries within itself and in its best traditions some portion of the spiritual treasure entrusted by God to humanity, even though many may not be aware of the source from which it comes.

87. International cooperation is needed today especially for those peoples who, besides facing so many other difficulties, likewise undergo pressures due to a rapid increase in population. There is an urgent need to explore, with the full and intense cooperation of all, and especially of the wealthier nations, ways whereby the human necessities of food and a suitable education can be furnished and shared with the entire human community. But some peoples could greatly improve upon the conditions of their life if they would change over from antiquated methods of farming to the new technical methods, applying them with needed prudence according to their own circumstances. Their life would likewise be improved by the establishment of a better social order and by a fairer system for the distribution of land ownership.

Governments undoubtedly have rights and duties, within the limits of their proper competency, regarding the population problem in their respective countries, for instance, with regard to social and family life legislation, or with regard to the migration of country-dwellers to the cities, or with respect to information concerning the condition and needs of the country. Since men today are giving thought to this problem and are so greatly disturbed over it, it is desirable in addition that Catholic specialists, especially in the universities, skillfully pursue and develop studies and projects on all these matters.

But there are many today who maintain that the increase in world population, or at least the population increase in some countries, must be radically curbed by every means possible and by any kind of intervention on the part of public authority. In view of this contention, the Council urges everyone to guard against solutions, whether publicly or privately supported, or at times even imposed, which are contrary to the moral law. For in keeping with man's inalienable right to marry and generate children, the decision concerning the number of children they will have depends on the correct judgment of the parents and it cannot in any way be left to the judgment of public authority. But since the judgment of the parents presupposes a rightly formed conscience, it is of the utmost importance that the way be open for everyone to develop a correct and genuinely human responsibility which respects the divine law and takes into consideration the circumstances of the place and the time. But sometimes this requires an improvement in educational and social conditions, and, above all, formation in religion or at least a complete moral training. Men should judiciously be informed, furthermore, of scientific advances in exploring methods whereby spouses can be helped in regulating the number of their children and whose safeness has been well proven and whose harmony with the moral order has been ascertained.

88.　Christians should cooperate willingly and wholeheartedly in establishing an international order that includes a genuine respect for all freedoms and amicable brotherhood between all. This is all the more pressing since the greater part of the world is still suffering from so much poverty that it is as if Christ Himself were crying out in these poor to beg the charity of the disciples. Do not let men, then, be scandalized because some countries with a majority of citizens who are counted as Christians have an abundance of wealth, whereas others are deprived of the necessities of life and are tormented with hunger, disease, and every kind of misery. The spirit of poverty and charity are the glory and witness of the Church of Christ.

Those Christians are to be praised and supported, therefore, who volunteer their services to help other men and nations. Indeed, it is the duty of the whole People of God, following the word and example of the bishops, to alleviate as far as they are able the sufferings of the modern age. They should do this too, as was the ancient custom in the Church, out of the substance of their goods, and not only out of what is superfluous.

The procedure of collecting and distributing aid, without being inflexible and completely uniform, should nevertheless be carried on in an orderly fashion in dioceses, nations, and throughout the entire world. Wherever it seems fitting, this activity of Catholics should be carried on in unison with other Christian brothers. For the spirit of charity does not forbid, but on the contrary commands that charitable activity be carried out in a careful and orderly manner. Therefore, it is essential for those who intend to dedicate themselves to the service of the developing nations to be properly trained in appropriate institutes.

89. Since, in virtue of her mission received from God, the Church preaches the Gospel to all men and dispenses the treasures of grace, she contributes to the ensuring of peace everywhere on earth and to the placing of the fraternal exchange between men on solid ground by imparting knowledge of the divine and natural law. Therefore, to encourage and stimulate cooperation among men, the Church must be clearly present in the midst of the community of nations, both through her official channels and through the full and sincere collaboration of all Christians—a collaboration motivated solely by the desire to be of service to all.

This will come about more effectively if the faithful themselves, conscious of their responsibility as men and as Christians, will exert their influence in their own milieu to arouse a ready willingness to cooperate with the international community. Special care must be given, in both religious and civic education, to the formation of youth in this regard.

90. An outstanding form of international activity on the part of Christians is found in the joint efforts which, both as individuals and in groups, they contribute to institutes already established or to be established for the encouragement of cooperation among nations. There are also various Catholic associations on the international level which can contribute in many ways to the building up of a peaceful and fraternal community of nations. These should be strengthened by augmenting in them the number of well qualified collaborators, by increasing needed resources, and by a suitable coordination of their forces. For today both effective action and the need for dialogue demand joint projects. Moreover, such associations contribute much to the development of a universal outlook—something certainly appropriate for Catholics. They also help to form an awareness of genuine universal solidarity and responsibility.

Finally, it is very much to be desired that Catholics, in order to fulfill their role properly in the international community, should seek to cooperate actively and in a positive manner both with their separated brothers, who together with them profess the Gospel of charity, and with all men thirsting for true peace.

The Council, considering the immensity of the hardships which still afflict the greater part of mankind today, regards it as most opportune that an organism of the universal Church be set up in order that both the justice and love of Christ toward the poor might be developed everywhere. The role of such an organism would be to stimulate the Catholic community to promote progress in needy regions and international social justice.

CONCLUSION

91. Drawn from the treasures of Church teaching, the proposals of this Sacred Synod look to the assistance of every man

of our time, whether he believes in God, or does not explicitly recognize Him. If adopted, they will promote among men a sharper insight into their full destiny, and thereby lead them to fashion the world more to man's surpassing dignity, to search for a brotherhood which is universal and more deeply rooted, and to meet the urgencies of our age with a gallant and unified effort born of love.

Undeniably this conciliar program is but a general one in several of its parts; and deliberately so, given the immense variety of situations and forms of human culture in the world. Indeed while it presents teaching already accepted in the Church, the program will have to be followed up and amplified since it sometimes deals with matters in a constant state of development. Still, we have relied on the word of God and the spirit of the Gospel. Hence we entertain the hope that many of our proposals will prove to be of substantial benefit to everyone, especially after they have been adapted to individual nations and mentalities by the faithful, under the guidance of their pastors.

92. By virtue of her mission to shed on the whole world the radiance of the Gospel message, and to unify under one Spirit all men of whatever nation, race or culture, the Church stands forth as a sign of that brotherhood which facilitates and invigorates sincere dialogue.

Such a mission requires in the first place that we foster within the Church itself mutual esteem, reverence and harmony, through the full recognition of lawful diversity. Thus all those who compose the one People of God, both pastors and the general faithful, can engage in dialogue with ever increasing effectiveness. For the bonds which unite the faithful are mightier than anything dividing them. Hence, let there be unity in essentials; freedom in doubtful matters; and in all things charity.

Our hearts embrace also those brothers and communities not yet living with us in full communion; to them we are linked nonetheless by our profession of the Father and the Son and the Holy Spirit, and by the bond of charity. We are not unmindful of the fact that the unity of Christians is today awaited and desired by many, too, who do not believe in Christ; for the further it advances toward truth and love under the powerful impulse of the Holy Spirit, the more this unity will be a harbinger of unity and peace for the world at large. Therefore, by common effort and in ways which are today increasingly appropriate for seeking this splendid goal effectively, let us take pains to pattern ourselves after the Gospel more exactly every day, and thus work as brothers in rendering service to the human family. For, in Christ Jesus this family is constituted to the family of the sons of God.

We think cordially too of all who acknowledge God, and who preserve in their traditions precious elements of religion and humanity. We want frank conversation to compel us all to receive the impulses of the Spirit faithfully and to act on them energetically.

For our part, the desire for such dialogue, which can lead to truth through love alone, excludes no one, though an appropriate measure of prudence must undoubtedly be exercised. We include those who cultivate outstanding qualities of the human spirit, but do not yet acknowledge the Source of these qualities. We include those who oppress the Church and harass her in manifold ways. Since God the Father is the origin and purpose of all men, we are all called to be brothers. Therefore, if we have been summoned to the same destiny, human and divine, we can and we should work together without violence and deceit in order to build up the world in genuine peace.

93. Mindful of the Lord's saying: "by this will all men know that you are my disciples, if you have love for one another" (John 13:35), Christians cannot yearn for anything more ardently than to serve the men of the modern world ever more generously and effectively. Therefore, by holding faithfully to the Gospel and benefiting from its resources, by joining with every man who loves and practices justice, Christians have shouldered a gigantic task to be carried out in this world, a task concerning which they must give a reckoning to Him who will judge every man on the last day.

Not everyone who cries, "Lord, Lord," will enter into the kingdom of heaven, but those who do the Father's will[1] by taking a strong grip on the work at hand. Now, the Father wills that in all men we recognize Christ our brother and love Him effectively, in word and in deed. By thus giving witness to the truth, we will share with others the mystery of the heavenly Father's love. As a consequence, men throughout the world will be aroused to a lively hope—the gift of the Holy Spirit—that finally they will be caught up in peace and utter happiness in that fatherland radiant with the glory of the Lord.

Now to Him who is able to accomplish all things in a measure far beyond what we ask or conceive, in keeping with the power that is at work in us—to Him be glory in the Church and in Christ Jesus, down through all the ages of time without end. Amen (Eph. 3:20-21).

❖ ❖ ❖ ❖

The entire text and all the individual elements which have been set forth in this Pastoral Constitution have pleased the Fathers. And by the Apostolic power conferred on us by Christ, we, together with the Venerable Fathers, in the Holy Spirit, approve, decree and enact them; and we order that what has been thus enacted in Council be promulgated, to the glory of God.

Rome, at St. Peter's, 7 December, 1965

I, PAUL, Bishop of the Catholic Church

There follow the signatures of the Fathers.

FOOTNOTES TO PREFACE

¹ The Pastoral Constitution *De Ecclesia in Mundo Huius Temporis* is made up of two parts; yet it constitutes an organic unity.

By way of explanation: the constitution is called "pastoral" because, while resting on doctrinal principles, it seeks to express the relation of the Church to the world and modern mankind. The result is that, on the one hand, a pastoral slant is present in the first part, and, on the other hand, a doctrinal slant is present in the second part.

In the first part, the Church develops her teaching on man, on the world which is the enveloping context of man's existence, and on man's relations to his fellow men. In part two, the Church gives closer consideration to various aspects of modern life and human society; special consideration is given to those questions and problems which, in this general area, seem to have a greater urgency in our day. As a result, in part two the subject matter which is viewed in the light of doctrinal principles is made up of diverse elements. Some elements have a permanent value; others, only a transitory one.

Consequently, the constitution must be interpreted according to the general norms of theological interpretation. Interpreters must bear in mind —especially in part two—the changeable circumstances which the subject matter, by its very nature, involves.

² Cf. John 18: 37; Matt. 20: 28; Mark. 10: 45.

INTRODUCTION

¹ Cf. Rom. 7: 14 ff.
² Cf. 2 Cor. 5: 15.
³ Cf. Acts 4: 12.
⁴ Cf. Heb. 13: 8.
⁵ Cf. Col. 1: 15.

PART I—CHAPTER 1

¹ Cf. Gen. 1: 26; Wis. 2: 23.
² Cf. Sir. 17: 3-10.
³ Cf. Rom. 1: 21-25.
⁴ Cf. John 8: 34.
⁵ Cf. Dan. 3: 57-90.
⁶ Cf. 1 Cor. 6: 13-20.
⁷ Cf. 1 Kings 16: 7; Jer. 17: 10.
⁸ Cf. Sir. 17: 7-8.
⁹ Cf. Rom. 2:14-16.
¹⁰ Cf. Pius XII, radio address on the correct formation of a Christian conscience in the young, March 23, 1952: AAS (1952), p. 271.
¹¹ Cf. Matt. 22: 37-40; Gal. 5: 14.
¹² Cf. Sir. 15: 14.
¹³ Cf. 2 Cor. 5: 10.
¹⁴ Cf. Wis. 1: 13; 2: 23-24; Rom. 5: 21; 6: 23; Jas. 1: 15.
¹⁵ Cf. 1 Cor. 15: 56-57.

[16] Cf. Pius XI, Encyclical Letter *Divini Redemptoris,* March 19, 1937: AAS 29 (1937), pp. 65-106; Pius XII, Encyclical Letter *Ad Apostolorum Principis,* June 29, 1958: AAS 50 (1958), pp. 601-614; John XXIII, Encyclical Letter *Mater et Magistra,* May 15, 1961: AAS 53 (1961), pp. 451-453; Paul VI, Encyclical Letter *Ecclesiam Suam,* Aug. 6, 1964: AAS 56 (1964), pp. 651-653.

[17] Cf. Second Vatican Council, *Dogmatic Constitution on the Church,* Chapter I, n. 8: AAS 57 (1965), p. 12.

[18] Cf. Phil. 1: 27.

[19] St. Augustine, *Confessions* I, 1: PL 32, 661.

[20] Cf. Rom. 5: 14. Cf. Tertullian, *De carnis resurrectione* 6: "The shape that the slime of the earth was given was intended with a view to Christ, the future man.": P. 2, 282; CSEL 47, p. 33, 1. 12-13.

[21] Cf. 2 Cor. 4: 4.

[22] Cf. Second Council of Constantinople, canon 7: "The divine Word was not changed into a human nature, nor was a human nature absorbed by the Word." Denzinger 219 (428).—Cf. also Third Council of Constantinople: "For just as His most holy and immaculate human nature, though deified, was not destroyed (theotheisa ouk anerethe), but rather remained in its proper state and mode of being": Denzinger 291 (556).—Cf. Council of Chalcedon: "to be acknowledged in two natures, without confusion, change, division, or separation." Denzinger 148 (302).

[23] Cf. Third Council of Constantinople: "and so His human will, though deified, is not destroyed": Denzinger 291 (556).

[24] Cf. Heb. 4: 15.

[25] Cf. 2 Cor. 5: 18-19; Col. 1: 20-22.

[26] Cf. 1 Pet. 2: 21; Matt. 16: 24; Luke 14: 27.

[27] Cf. Rom. 8: 29; Col. 1: 18.

[28] Cf. Rom. 8: 1-11.

[29] Cf. 2 Cor. 4: 14.

[30] Cf. Phil. 3: 10; Rom. 8: 17.

[31] Cf. Second Vatican Council, *Dogmatic Constitution on the Church,* Chapter 2, n. 16: AAS 57 (1965), p. 20.

[32] Cf. Rom. 8: 32.

[33] Cf. The Byzantine Easter Liturgy.

[34] Cf. Rom. 8: 15 and Gal. 4: 6; cf. also John 1: 12 and John 3: 1-2.

PART I—CHAPTER 2

[1] Cf. John XXIII, Encyclical Letter *Mater et Magistra,* May 15, 1961: AAS 53 (1961), pp. 401-464, and Encyclical Letter *Pacem in Terris,* April 11, 1963: AAS 55 (1963), pp. 257-304; Paul VI, Encyclical Letter *Ecclesiam Suam,* Aug. 6, 1964: AAS 54 (1964), pp. 609-659.

[2] Cf. Luke 17: 33.

[3] Cf. St. Thomas, 1 *Ethica Lect.* 1.

[4] Cf. John XXIII, Encyclical Letter *Mater et Magistra:* AAS 53 (1961), p. 418. Cf. also Pius XI, Encyclical Letter *Quadragesimo Anno:* AAS 23 (1931), p. 222 ff.

⁵ Cf. John XXIII, Encyclical Letter *Mater et Magistra:* AAS 53 (1961).
⁶ Cf. Mark 2: 27.
⁷ Cf. John XXIII, Encyclical Letter *Pacem in Terris:* AAS 55 (1963), p. 266.
⁸ Cf. Jas. 2: 15-16.
⁹ Cf. Luke 16: 19-31.
¹⁰ Cf. John XXIII, Encyclical Letter *Pacem in Terris:* AAS 55 (1963), p. 299 and 300.
¹¹ Cf. Luke 6: 37-38; Matt. 7: 1-2; Rom. 2: 1-11; 14: 10; 14: 10-12.
¹² Cf. Matt. 5: 43-47.
¹³ Cf. *Dogmatic Constitution on the Church,* Chapter II, n. 9: AAS 57 (1965). pp. 12-13.
¹⁴ Cf. Exodus 24: 1-8.

PART I—CHAPTER 3

¹ Cf. Gen. 1: 26-27; 9: 2-3; Wis. 9: 3.
² Cf. Ps. 8: 7 and 10.
³ Cf. John XXIII, Encyclical Letter *Pacem in Terris:* AAS 55 (1963), p. 297.
⁴ Cf. message to all mankind sent by the Fathers at the beginning of the Second Vatican Council, Oct. 20, 1962: AAS 54 (1962), p. 823.
⁵ Cf. Paul VI, address to the diplomatic corps, Jan. 7, 1965: AAS 57 (1965), p. 232.
⁶ Cf. First Vatican Council, *Dogmatic Constitution on the Catholic Faith,* Chapter III: Denz. 1785-1786 (3004-3005).
⁷ Cf. Msgr. Pio Paschini, *Vita e opere di Galileo Galilei,* 2 volumes, Vatican Press (1964).
⁸ Cf. Matt. 24: 13; 13: 24-30 and 36-43.
⁹ Cf. 2 Cor. 6: 10.
¹⁰ Cf. John 1: 3 and 14.
¹¹ Cf. Eph. 1: 10.
¹² Cf. John 3: 6; Rom. 5: 8-10.
¹³ Cf. Acts 2: 36; Matt. 28: 18.
¹⁴ Cf. Rom. 15: 16.
¹⁵ Cf. Acts 1: 7.
¹⁶ Cf. 1 Cor. 7: 31; St. Irenaeus, *Adversus haereses,* V, 36, PG, VIII, 1221.
¹⁷ Cf. 2 Cor. 5: 2; 2 Pet. 3: 13.
¹⁸ Cf. 1 Cor. 2: 9; Apoc. 21: 4-5.
¹⁹ Cf. 1 Cor. 15: 42 and 53.
²⁰ Cf. 1 Cor. 13: 8; 3: 14.
²¹ Cf. Rom. 8: 19-21.
²² Cf. Luke 9: 25.
²³ Cf. Pius XI, Encyclical Letter *Quadragesimo Anno:* AAS 23 (1931), p. 207.
²⁴ Preface of the Feast of Christ the King.

¹ Cf. Paul VI, Encyclical Letter *Ecclesiam suam*, III: AAS 56 (1964), pp. 637-659.

² Cf. Titus 3: 4: "love of mankind."

³ Cf. Eph. 1: 3; 5-6; 13-14, 23.

⁴ Second Vatican Council, *Dogmatic Constitution on the Church*, Chapter I, n. 8: AAS 57 (1965), p. 12.

⁵ *Ibid.*, Chapter II, no. 9: AAS 57 (1965), p. 14; Cf. n. 8: AAS *loc. cit.*, p. 11.

⁶ *Ibid.*, Chapter I, n. 8: AAS 57 (1965), pp. 11.

⁷ Cf. *ibid.*, Chapter IV, n. 38: AAS 57 (1965), p. 43, with note 120.

⁸ Cf. Rom. 8: 14-17.

⁹ Cf. Matt. 22: 39.

¹⁰ *Dogmatic Constitution on the Church*, Chapter II, n. 9: AAS 57 (1956), pp. 12-14.

¹¹ Cf. Pius XII, Address to the International Union of Institutes of Archeology, History and History of Art, March 9, 1956: AAS 48 (1956), p. 212: "Its divine Founder, Jesus Christ, has not given it any mandate or fixed any end of the cultural order. The goal which Christ assigns to it is strictly religious . . . The Church must lead men to God, in order that they may be given over to him without reserve. . . . The Church can never lose sight of the strictly religious, supernatural goal. The meaning of all its activities, down to the last canon of its Code, can only cooperate directly or indirectly in this goal."

¹² *Dogmatic Constitution on the Church*, Chapter I, n. 1: AAS 57 (1965), p. 5.

¹³ Cf. Heb. 13: 14.

¹⁴ Cf. 2 Thes. 3: 6-13; Eph. 4: 28.

¹⁵ Cf. Is. 58: 1-12.

¹⁶ Cf. Matt. 23: 3-23; Mark 7: 10-13.

¹⁷ Cf. John XXIII, Encyclical Letter *Mater et Magistra*, IV: AAS 53 (1961), pp. 456-457; cf. I: AAS *loc. cit.*, pp. 407, 410-411.

¹⁸ Cf. *Dogmatic Constitution on the Church*, Chapter III, n. 28: AAS 57 (1965), p. 35.

¹⁹ *Ibid.*, n. 28: AAS *loc. cit.*, pp. 35-36.

²⁰ Cf. St. Ambrose, *De virginitate*, Chapter VIII, n. 48: ML 16, 278.

²¹ Cf. *Dogmatic Constitution on the Church*, Chapter II, n. 15: AAS 57 (1965), p. 20.

²² Cf. *Dogmatic* ᵕnstitution *on the Church*, Chapter II, n. 13: AAS 57 (1965), p. 17.

²³ Cf. Justin, *Dialogus cum Tryphene*, Chapter 110; MG 6, 729 (ed. Otto), 1897, pp. 391-393: ". . . but the greater the number of persecutions which are inflicted upon us, so much the greater the number of other men who become devout believers through the name of Jesus." Cf. Tertullian, *Apologeticus*, Chapter L, 13: "Every time you mow us down like grass, we increase in number: the blood of Christians is a seed!" Cf. *Dogmatic Constitution on the Church*, Chapter II, n. 9: AAS 57 (1965), p. 14.

[21] Cf. *Dogmatic Constitution on the Church,* Chapter II, n. 15: AAS 57 (1965), p. 20.

[25] Cf. Paul VI, address given on Feb. 3, 1965.

PART II—CHAPTER 1

[1] Cf. St. Augustine, *De Bene coniugali* PL 40, 375-376 and 394; St. Thomas, *Summa Theologica,* Suppl. Quaest. 49, art. 3 ad 1; *Decretum pro Armenis:* Denz.-Schoen. 1327; Pius XI, Encyclical Letter *Casti Connubii:* AAS 22 (1930, pp. 547-548; Denz.-Schoen. 3703-3714.

[2] Cf. Pius XI, Encyclical Letter *Casti Connubii:* AAS 22 (1930), pp. 546-547; Denz.-Schoen. 3706.

[3] Cf. Osee 2; Jer. 3: 6-13; Ezech. 16 and 23; Is. 54.

[4] Cf. Matt. 9: 15; Mark 2: 19-20; Luke 5: 34-35; John 3: 29; cf. also 2 Cor. 11: 2; Eph. 5: 27; Apoc. 19: 7-8; 21: 2 and 9.

[5] Cf. Eph. 5: 25.

[6] Cf. Second Vatican Council, *Dogmatic Constitution on the Church:* AAS 57 (1965), pp. 15-16; 40-41; 47.

[7] Pius XI, Encyclical Letter *Casti Connubii:* AAS 22 (1930), p. 583.

[8] Cf. 1 Tim. 5: 3.

[9] Cf. Eph. 5: 32.

[10] Cf. Gen. 2: 22-24; Prov. 5: 18-20; 31: 10-31; Tob. 8: 4-8; Cant. 1: 2-3; 2: 16; 4: 16-5: 1; 7: 8-11; 1 Cor. 7: 3-6; Eph. 5: 25-33.

[11] Cf. Pius XI, Encyclical Letter *Casti Connubii:* AAS 22 (1930), p. 547 and 548; Denz.-Schoen. 3707.

[12] Cf. 1 Cor. 7: 5.

[13] Cf. Pius XII, Address, *Tra le visite,* Jan. 20, 1958: AAS 50 (1958), p. 91.

[14] Cf. Pius XI, Encyclical Letter *Casti Connubii:* AAS 22 (1930): Denz.-Schoen. 3716-3718; Pius XII, *Allocutio Conventui Unionis Italicae inter Obstetrices,* Oct. 29, 1951: AAS 43 (1951), pp. 835-854; Paul VI, address to a group of cardinals, June 23, 1964: AAS 56 (1964), pp. 581-589. Certain questions which need further and more careful investigation have been handed over, at the command of the Supreme Pontiff, to a commission for the study of population, family, and births, in order that, after it fulfills its function, the Supreme Pontiff may pass judgment. Since the doctrine of the magisterium is such, this holy Synod does not intend to propose immediately concrete solutions.

[15] Cf. Eph. 5: 16; Col. 4: 5.

[16] Cf. *Sacramentarium Gregorianum:* PL 78, 262.

[17] Cf. Rom. 5: 15 and 18; 6: 5-11; Gal. 2: 20.

[18] Cf. Eph. 5: 25-27.

PART II—CHAPTER 2

[1] Cf. Introductory statement of this constitution, n. 4 ff.

[2] Cf. Col. 3: 1-2.

[3] Cf. Gen. 1: 28.

[4] Cf. Prov. 8: 30-31.

⁵ Cf. St. Irenaeus, *Adversus haereses*, III, 11, 8 (ed. Sagnard, p. 200; cf. *ibid.*, 16, 6: pp. 290-292; 21, 10-22: pp. 370-372; 22, 3: p. 378; etc.)

⁶ Cf. Eph. 1: 10.

⁷ Cf. the words of Pius XI to Father M. D. Roland-Gosselin: "It is necessary never to lose sight of the fact that the objective of the Church is to evangelize, not to civilize. If it civilizes, it is for the sake of evangelization." (Semaines sociales de France, Versailles, 1936, pp. 461-462).

⁸ First Vatican Council, *Constitution on the Catholic Faith:* Denzinger 1795, 1799 (3015, 3019). Cf. Pius XI, Encyclical Letter *Quadragesimo Anno:* AAS 23 (1931), p. 190.

⁹ Cf. John XXIII, Encyclical Letter *Pacem in Terris:* AAS 55 (1963), p. 260.

¹⁰ Cf. John XXIII, Encyclical Letter *Pacem in Terris:* AAS 55 (1963), p. 283; Pius XII, radio address, Dec. 24, 1941: AAS 34 (1942), pp. 16-17.

¹¹ John XXIII, Encyclical Letter *Pacem in Terris:* AAS 55 (1963), p. 260.

¹² Cf. John XXIII, prayer delivered on Oct. 11, 1962, at the beginning of the Council: AAS 54 (1962), p. 792.

¹³ Cf. *Constitution on the Sacred Liturgy*, n. 123: AAS 56 (1964), p. 131; Paul VI, discourse to the artists of Rome: AAS 56 (1964), pp. 439-442.

¹⁴ Cf. Second Vatican Council, *Decree on Priestly Training* and *Declaration on Christian Education.*

¹⁵ Cf. *Dogmatic Constitution on the Church*, Chapter IV, n. 37: AAS 57 (1965), pp. 42-43.

PART II—CHAPTER 3

¹ Cf. Pius XII, address on March 23, 1952: AAS 44 (1953), p. 273; John XXIII, allocution to the Catholic Association of Italian Workers, May 1, 1959: AAS 51 (1959), p. 358.

² Cf. Pius XI, Encyclical Letter *Quadragesimo Anno:* AAS 23 (1931), p. 190 ff. Pius XII, address of March 23, 1952: AAS 44 (1952), p. 276 ff; John XXIII, Encyclical Letter *Mater et Magistra:* AAS 53 (1961), p. 450; Vatican Council II, *Decree on the Media of Social Communication*, Chapter I, n. 6: AAS 56 (1964), p. 147.

³ Cf. Matt. 16: 26; Luke 16: 1-31; Col. 3: 17.

⁴ Cf. Leo XIII, Encyclical Letter *Libertas*, in *Acta Leonis XIII*, t. VIII, p. 220 ff; Pius XI, Encyclical Letter *Quadragesimo Anno:* AAS 23 (1931), p. 191 ff; Pius XI, Encyclical Letter *Divini Redemptoris:* AAS 39 (1937), p. 65 ff; Pius XII, *Nuntius natalicius 1941:* AAS 34 (1942), p. 10 ff; John XXIII, Encyclical Letter *Mater et Magistra:* AAS 53 (1961), pp. 401-464.

⁵ In reference to agricultural problems cf. especially John XXIII, Encyclical Letter *Mater et Magistra:* AAS 53 (1961), p. 341 ff.

⁶ Cf. Leo XIII, Encyclical Letter *Rerum Novarum:* AAS 23 (1890-91), p. 649, p. 662; Pius XI, Encyclical Letter *Quadragesimo Anno:* AAS 23 (1931), pp. 200-201; Pius XI, Encyclical Letter *Divini Redemptoris:* AAS 29 (1937), p. 92; Pius XII, radio address on Christmas Eve, 1942: AAS 35 (1943), p. 20; Pius XII, allocution of June 13, 1943: AAS 35 (1943), p.

172; Pius XII, radio address to the workers of Spain, March 11, 1951: AAS 43 (1951), p. 215; John XXIII, Encyclical Letter *Mater et Magistra:* AAS 53 (1961), p. 419.

[7] Cf. John XXIII, Encyclical Letter *Mater et Magistra:* AAS 53 (1961), pp. 408, 424, 427; however, the word "curatione" has been taken from the Latin text of the Encyclical Letter *Quadragesimo Anno:* AAS 23 (1931), p. 199. Under the aspect of the evolution of the question cf. also: Pius XII, allocution of June 3, 1950: AAS 42 (1950), pp. 485-488; Paul VI, allocution of June 8, 1964: AAS 56 (1964), pp. 574-579.

[8] Cf. Pius XII, Encyclical *Sertum Laetitiae:* AAS 31 (1939), p. 642; John XXIII, consistorial allocution: AAS 52 (1960), pp. 5-11; John XXIII, Encyclical Letter *Mater et Magistra:* AAS 53 (1961), p. 411.

[9] Cf. St. Thomas, *Summa Theologica:* II-II, q. 32, a. 5 ad 2; *Ibid.* q. 66, a. 2: cf. explanation in Leo XIII, Encyclical Letter *Rerum Novarum:* AAS 23 (1890-91) p. 651; cf. also Pius XII, allocution of June 1, 1941: AAS 33 (1941), p. 199; Pius XII, birthday radio address 1954: AAS 47 (1955), p. 27.

[10] Cf. St. Basil, *Hom. in illud Lucae "Destruam horrea mea,"* n. 2 (PG 31, 263); Lactantius, *Divinarum institutionum,* lib. V. on justice (PL 6, 565 B); St. Augustine, *In Ioann. Ev.* tr. 50, n. 6 (PL 35, 1760); St. Augustine, *Enarratio in Ps.* CXLVII, 12 (PL 37, 192); St. Gregory the Great, *Homiliae in Ev.,* hom. 20 (PL 76, 1165); St. Gregory the Great, *Regulae Pastoralis liber,* pars III, c. 21 (PL 77, 87); St. Bonaventure, *In III Sent.* d. 33, dub. 1 (ed Quaracchi, III, 728); St. Bonaventure, *In IV Sent.* d. 15, p. II, a.2 q.1 (ed. cit. IV, 371 b); q. de superfluo (ms. Assisi, Bibl. Comun. 186, ff. 112ª-113ª); St. Albert the Great, *In III Sent.,* d. 33, a.3, sol. 1 (ed. Borgnet XXVIII, 611); Id. *In IV Sent.* d. 15, a. 16 (ed. cit. XXIX, 494-497). As for the determination of what is superfluous in our day and age, cf. John XXIII, radio-television message of Sept. 11, 1962: AAS 54 (1962) p. 682: "The obligation of every man, the urgent obligation of the Christian man, is to reckon what is superfluous by the measure of the needs of others, and to see to it that the administration and the distribution of created goods serve the common good."

[11] In that case, the old principle holds true: "In extreme necessity all goods are common, that is, all goods are to be shared." On the other hand, for the order, extension, and manner by which the principle is applied in the proposed text, besides the modern authors: cf. St. Thomas, *Summa Theologica* II-II, q. 66, a. 7. Obviously, for the correct application of the principle, all the conditions that are morally required must be met.

[12] Cf. Gratian, *Decretum, C.* 21, dist. LXXXVI (ed. Friedberg I, 302). This axiom is also found already in PL 54, 591 A (cf. in Antonianum 27 (1952) 349-366).

[13] Cf. Leo XIII, Encyclical Letter *Rerum Novarum:* AAS 23 (1890-91), pp. 643-646; Pius XI, Encyclical Letter *Quadragesimo Anno:* AAS 23 (1931), p. 191; Pius XII, radio message of June 1, 1941: AAS 33 (1941), p. 199; Pius XII, radio message on Christmas Eve 1942: AAS 35 (1943), p. 17; Pius XII, radio message of Sept. 1, 1944: AAS 36(1944), p. 253; John XXIII, Encyclical Letter *Mater et Magistra:* AAS 53 (1961), pp. 428-429.

¹⁴ Cf. Pius XI, Encyclical Letter *Quadragesimo Anno:* AAS 23 (1931), p. 214; John XXIII, Encyclical Letter *Mater et Magistra:* AAS 53 (1961), p. 429.

¹⁵ Cf. Pius XII, radio message of Pentecost 1941: AAS 44 (1941), p. 199; John XXIII, Encyclical Letter *Mater et Magistra:* AAS 53 (1961), p. 430.

¹⁶ For the right use of goods according to the doctrine of the New Testament, cf. Luke 3: 11; 10: 30 ff; 11: 41; 1 Pet. 5: 3; Mark 8: 36; 12: 39-41; Jas. 5: 1-6; 1 Tim. 6: 8; Eph. 4: 28; 2 Cor. 8: 13; 1 John 3: 17 ff.

PART II—CHAPTER 4

¹ Cf. John XXIII, Encyclical Letter *Mater et Magistra:* AAS 53 (1961), p. 417.

² Cf. John XXIII, *ibid.*

³ Cf. Rom. 13: 1-5.

⁴ Cf. Rom. 13: 5.

⁵ Cf. Pius XII, radio message, Dec. 24, 1942: AAS 35 (1943), pp. 9-24; Dec. 24, 1944: AAS 37 (1945), pp. 11-17; John XXIII, Encyclical Letter *Pacem In Terris:* AAS 55 (1963), pp. 263, 271, 277 and 278.

⁶ Cf. Pius XII, radio message of June 7, 1941: AAS 33 (1941), p. 200; John XXIII, Encyclical Letter *Pacem in Terris:* l.c., p. 273 and 274.

⁷ Cf. John XXIII, Encyclical Letter *Mater et Magistra:* AAS 53 (1961), p. 416.

⁸ Pius XI, allocution "Ai dirigenti della Federazione Universitaria Cattolica". *Discorsi di Pio XI* (ed. Bertetto), Turin, vol. 1 (1960), p. 743.

⁹ Cf. Second Vatican Council, *Dogmatic Constitution on the Church,* n. 13: AAS 57 (1965), p. 17.

¹⁰ Cf. Luke 2: 14.

PART II—CHAPTER 5

¹ Eph. 2: 16; Col. 1: 20-22.

² Cf. John XXIII, Encyclical Letter *Pacem in Terris,* April 11, 1963: AAS 55 (1963), p. 291: "Therefore in this age of ours which prides itself on its atomic power, it is irrational to believe that war is still an apt means of vindicating violated rights."

³ Cf. Pius XII, allocution of Sept. 30, 1954: AAS 46 (1954), p. 589; radio message of Dec. 24, 1954: AAS 47 (1955), pp. 15 ff; John XXIII, Encyclical Letter *Pacem in Terris:* AAS 55 (1963), pp. 286-291; Paul VI, allocution to the United Nations, Oct. 4, 1965.

⁴ Cf. John XXIII, Encyclical Letter *Pacem in Terris,* where reduction of arms is mentioned: AAS 55 (1963), p. 287.

⁵ Cf. 2 Cor. 2: 6.

CONCLUSION

¹ Cf. Matt. 7: 21.

DISCUSSION OUTLINE

by REV. DONALD R. CAMPION, S.J.

(Numbers in parentheses refer to paragraphs, not pages)

Preface (1-3)

1. Why does the Church feel truly linked with mankind? (1)
2. Which of its other documents does the Council regard as an introduction to this pastoral constitution? (2)
3. What will be the focal point of the entire constitution? Why? (3)

Introductory Statement (4-10)

4. Why must the Church study the "signs of the times"? (4)
5. What are some difficulties that accompany the dramatic advances of our age? (4)
6. What forces prompted men to adopt a "more dynamic, evolutionary concept" of reality? (5)
7. What are some of the major social movements of our day? Are they found only in the more developed nations? (6)
8. How has social change influenced young people? (7)
9. What have been the good and bad results of the impact of recent social changes in religion? (7)
10. Why is man "at once the cause and victim" of mutual distrust and enmities in today's world? (8)
11. In what areas do men today especially demand an end to injustice and inequality? (9)
12. How do you define the "more basic imbalance" with which the modern world's other imbalances are linked? (10)
13. Where does the Church find the key to all answers to questions on the nature and destiny of man? (10)

PART I: THE CHURCH AND MAN'S CALLING (11-45)

14. Who are the People of God and what is their mission to the human race? (11)
15. What are the two extremes in modern man's viewing of himself? (12)

CHAPTER I: THE DIGNITY OF THE
HUMAN PERSON (12-22)

16. How does the Council decide the relationship between men and women? (12)
17. Why is man split within himself and what are the consequences of this split? (13)
18. Is man supposed to despise his bodily life? Where does he discern his proper destiny? (14)
19. Is man's intelligence confined to knowledge of observable data? (15)
20. Why is wisdom especially necessary to man today? Are the rich nations today always the wiser ones? (15)
21. How do you define the voice of conscience? Why is it the sanctuary of a man? (16)
22. Why does the act of man's conscience make it necessary that man be free? (17)
23. Why does man rebel against death? How does the Christian faith answer man's anxieties about the mystery of death? (18)
24. What is the root explanation of human dignity? (19)
25. Is there only one brand of atheism? Does it have anything to do with false ideas of God or the existence of social evil? (19)
26. How can it be said that believers themselves frequently bear responsibility for some forms of atheism? (19)
27. In what way does modern technical progress contribute to belief in modern systematic atheism? (20)
28. Why do some atheists hold that religion acts as an opiate and thus blocks economic and social progress? (20)
29. What are some of the Church's documents which had rejected modern atheism? (21)
30. Why does the Vatican Council insist that an effective answer to atheism must involve both doctrine and practice or works? (21)
31. Why does the Church protest against state discrimination between believers and unbelievers? What does such discrimination do to dialogue? (21)

32. How has the Incarnation united Christ with every man? (22)
33. Is a link with the paschal mystery possible for those who are not Christians? If so how? (22)

CHAPTER II: THE COMMUNITY OF MANKIND (23-32)

34. What is the name also used by the Council to describe the "growing interdependence of men"? (23)
35. What are some classic documents that have set forth the Church's social doctrine? (23)
36. What basis is there for the claim that God wills men to be one family? Is the nature of human unity in any way revealed in the life of God Himself? (24)
37. How can man's selfishness harm the social order? How does the social order or environment influence man's life? (25)
38. How do you define the "common good"? (26)
39. What are some rights that are based on the dignity of the human person? (26)
40. What are the four components of a sound social order? (26)
41. Who are the special persons that the Council warns us to look on as our neighbors? (27)
42. What does the Council have to say about what violates human life, the integrity of the human person or human dignity? (27)
43. What attitudes should we have toward those who differ from us or oppose us? (28)
44. How does the Council argue to the unity of men and their equal dignity? (29)
45. Does the Council reject all differences among men? (29)
46. What does the Council say about "individualistic morality"? How does it look on those who violate health or traffic regulations of the State? (30)
47. Why is universal education particularly necessary today? (31)
48. Does the Council have anything to say on universal suffrage? (31)

49. What does the Council have to say about the communitarian or collective character of salvation? Does it still exist? (32)

CHAPTER III: MAN'S ACTIVITY THROUGHOUT THE WORLD (33-39)

50. Does increased social contact lead to recognition of the existence of a single world community? (33)
51. Does belief in the Christian message restrict or encourage involvement in efforts to master the secrets of the universe? (34)
52. Why is man "more precious for what he is than for what he has"? What does this tell us about the relative importance of technical progress and the quest for better human relations in the world? (35)
53. Does the Council foresee inevitable conflicts between faith and scientific inquiry? What does it have to say about such episodes as the famous Galileo case? (36)
54. What practical lesson does the Council draw from the fact of the struggle with the powers of darkness that runs through all of man's history? How can Christians live in the world and yet follow St. Paul's warning to "be not conformed to this world"? (37)
55. How does the event of the Resurrection influence a Christian's attitude toward the present life and the world in which he finds himself? How is this view confirmed by the Eucharist? (38)
56. What is the relationship between the growth of Christ's Kingdom and earthly progress? (39)

CHAPTER IV: THE ROLE OF THE CHURCH IN THE MODERN WORLD (40-45)

57. Why does the Council speak of the Church as "a kind of soul for human society"? (40)
58. How does the Catholic Church view the contributions of other Christian Churches to the family of man? (40)
59. What are some opinions which threaten the dignity of man and which the Church resists? (41)

60. How does the Church look on today's dynamic movements on behalf of human rights? (41)

61. What is there in the Church's mission and nature that qualifies it particularly to strengthen bonds between nations? (42)

62. What are the basic freedoms the Church asks for itself from any form of civil government? (42)

63. What possible errors does the Council caution against in the thinking of Christians insofar as they are "citizens of two cities"? (43)

64. What are the special responsibilities of laymen in the world? Should they normally look to their pastors for concrete solutions to problems confronting them? (43)

65. What are the responsibilities of priests and bishops in the social order? (43)

66. How does the Council look on past failings and infidelities of clergy and laity? Does it judge that the Church must learn from historical experience? (43)

67. What are some areas of human experience and achievement from which the Church can profit? How can she learn about her nature from a contact with other social institutions? (44)

PART II: SOME PROBLEMS OF SPECIAL URGENCY (46-95)

68. Which are the subjects of universal concern today that the Council chooses to explore? (46)

CHAPTER I: FOSTERING THE NOBILITY OF MARRIAGE AND THE FAMILY (47-52)

69. What are the particular developments that today threaten marriage and family, or trouble consciences? (47)

70. Why does the Council speak of marriage as a covenant of many-faceted love? How is authentic married love related to divine love? (48)

71. How do children contribute to making their parents holy? (48)

72. How is conjugal love seen as a merging of the human with the divine? (49)

73. How does the Council describe the relation between conjugal love and the begetting and educating of children? Does it give procreation priority over the other purposes of matrimony? (50)

74. What circumstances must parents consider before undertaking the responsibility of new parenthood? Who should make the judgment here? (50)

75. Does the Council recognize circumstances where the size of a family should not be increased? What does the Council say about dishonorable methods of birth regulation? (51)

76. How does the Council describe the role of parents in the training of children? Is a mother's activities to be confined to the home? (52)

77. What are the responsibilities of the state, of scientists and of priests toward family life? Does the Council have anything to say on groups such as the Christian Family Movement? (52)

CHAPTER II: THE DEVELOPMENT OF CULTURE (53-62)

78. How is culture defined in its general sense? In what senses may one speak of a plurality of human cultures? (53)

79. What are some of the particular characteristics of culture today? (54)

80. What is the keynote of the new humanism of our age? (55)

81. In man's quest for the advance of culture today, what seemingly contradictory values must be simultaneously safeguarded? (56)

82. Can man fulfill God's will by involving himself in shaping human society or the pursuit of modern science? (57)

83. What are some of the positive values in modern scientifically oriented culture and what are some of the perils? (57)

84. How is the Church at one and the same time necessarily linked to contemporary culture and yet not indissolubly tied to any one way of life? (58)

85. Why must culture exercise its own autonomy? Had any previous Council recognized such autonomy of human arts and disciplines? (59)

86. What attitude does the Council take toward subordination of culture to an ideology? (59)

87. Which groups in society today need special help in order to participate adequately in the advance of culture? (60)

88. What alternative does the Council urge in place of the disappearing image of the "universal man"? (61)

89. What values does the Council see in sports and tourism as legitimate uses of man's newly acquired mass leisure? (61)

90. Does the Council look on the advances of modern science and philosophy as a threat or a challenge? What sort of relationship does it call for between the theologian and the scientist or artist? (62)

91. In what sense can the Council now be said to have proclaimed a Bill of Rights for intellectuals in the Church? (62)

CHAPTER III: ECONOMIC AND SOCIAL LIFE (63-72)

92. What paradoxes does the Council see following in the wake of modern economic developments? (63)

93. Are many today willing to put up with economic and social inequalities as inevitable consequences of man's condition? (63)

94. How does the Council define the fundamental purpose of increased economic production? How does this relate to its basic approach to all social problems? (64)

95. What importance does the Council attach to broad sharing in the management of economic enterprises? (65)

96. Why does the Council regard individualism and collectivism as errors? (66)

97. What norm does the Council offer for a just adjustment to the onset of automation in industry? (66)

98. What are the bases for asserting the dignity of human labor? What norms must be observed in organizing and directing workers? (67)

99. How does the principle of participation in decision-making apply to labor-management relations in the economic community? (68)

100. What does the Council teach on the right to organize, to bargain collectively and to strike? (68)

101. In what sense is there a common destiny for all goods and property on the earth? What does this suggest with respect to such questions as foreign aid by rich nations? (69)

102. Must systems of common ownership of property always be changed to private ownership in a soundly organized society or country? (69)

103. What should be the aims of a just investment policy? (70)

104. What are the arguments adduced by the Council in support of the traditional concept of private property? (71)

105. Why does the Council insist that land reforms are so necessary in some parts of the world? (71)

106. What role does the Council expect Christians to play in the fight for justice and charity in the world today? (72)

CHAPTER IV: THE LIFE OF THE POLITICAL COMMUNITY (73-76)

107. What accounts for the keen interest today in providing better guarantees of human rights? Is there a similar concern over the rights of minority groups? (73)

108. What is the purpose of a political community? Why must there be a system of authority in it? (74)

109. What limits exist on any political authority? What right do citizens have to defend themselves against abuses of authority? (74)

110. How does the Council look on representative government? Why does it support a division of functions in government and independent safeguards of citizens' rights? (75)

111. What formula does the Council provide for harmony in a pluralistic society? How does it speak of the art of politics? (75)

112. How does the Council conceive of a proper relationship between Church and State? Does it conflict in any way with the general constitutional consensus in the United States on Church-State relations (76)

113. Why is the Church willing to renounce the exercise of her legitimate rights at times? What rights must she always claim for herself and why? (76)

CHAPTER V: THE FOSTERING OF PEACE AND THE PROMOTION OF A COMMUNITY OF NATIONS (77-90)

114. What constitutes the "hour of supreme crisis" confronting the whole human family today? (77)

115. Why does the Council state that peace is the fruit of both justice and love? (78)

116. What attitude does the Council take toward those who follow a philosophy of nonviolence in vindicating their rights? (78)

117. How does the Council view the argument that those under authority are not responsible for criminal actions commanded by superiors? What recent events of history make such a judgment relevant for modern men? (79)

118. Is the reference in the text to conscientious objectors an affirmation of their reasons for their stand or does it by-pass that issue? (79)

119. Do governments have the right to legitimate self-defense? How should those in the military service of their country normally regard themselves? (79)

120. Why does the Council judge that it must evaluate war with an entirely new attitude? (80)

121. What moral judgment is to be made on obliteration bombing of cities? (80)

122. What potential evil does the Council see arising from the possession by nations of new scientific weapons? (80)

123. Does the Council entirely rule out possession of modern weapons for purposes of deterrence? How does it view the present arms race? What group is particularly damaged by the arms race even in times of peace? (81)

124. What goal must be sought with regard to modern war? What should be the concerns of statesmen in this regard? (82)

125. Can individual citizens leave the effort for peace to their government officials? How can they exercise their own influence here? (82)

126. What are some of the root causes of discord among nations? (83)

127. Why are international organizations particularly necessary today? What services must they provide? (84)

128. What are some aims or attitudes that threaten the construction of a satisfactory international economic order? (85)

129. What are some obligations of the developing and advanced nations, respectively, with regard to international economic cooperation? (86)

130. How does the principle of subsidiarity apply in the international economic community? (86)

131. How does the rapid increase in population of some nations affect the working of the international economic order? (87)

132. May governments formulate national population policy and programs? What are some improper forms of public intervention in this area? (87)

133. Why does the Council insist that it is parents who have the right and duty to decide concerning the number of children they will have? What sort of information about regulating the number of children in a family should be furnished to parents? (87)

134. What types of aid and service to other men and nations does the Council propose for individual Christians and for dioceses or national groups? (88)

135. How should the Church be present in the midst of the community of nations? (89)

136. Why should Catholics find it particularly appropriate to participate in joint projects for international affairs? Should there be an ecumenical dimension to such cooperation? (90)

137. What practical proposal does the Council make to stimulate the universal Church's efforts toward international social justice? (90)

138. What general results does the Council expect from an adoption of its proposals by men of good will? (91)
139. Does the Council claim to offer new teaching to any great degree in this constitution? (91)
140. What attitudes must be fostered within the Church itself if it is to be a sign of brotherhood and thus act to advance sincere dialogue? (92)
141. Who are considered to be suitable partners for dialogue? Does the Council exclude any one or any group from its hopes for dialogue? (92)
142. How should Christians look on the chances to serve men of the modern world? (93)
143. What was the date on which this pastoral constitution was solemnly voted and promulgated? Who were the signers of the document? (93)

BIBLIOGRAPHY

by REV. DONALD R. CAMPION, S. J.

Balthasar, Hans Urs von: *A Theology of History* (Sheed and Ward).

Barrett, Donald N. (ed.): *The Problem of Population: Moral and Theological Considerations* (U. of Notre Dame Press).

Bea, Augustin Cardinal: *The Unity of Christians* (Herder and Herder).

Bromley, Dorothy D.: *Catholics and Birth Control: Contemporary Views on Doctrine* (Devin-Adair).

Calvez, Jean-Yves, and Perrin, Jacques: *The Church and Social Justice: Papal Social Teaching from Leo XIII to Pius XII* (Regnery).

Calvez, Jean-Yves: *The Social Thought of John XXIII* (Regnery).

Carillo de Albornoz, A. F.: *Roman Catholicism and Religious Liberty* (World Council of Churches, Geneva).

Cavanagh, John R.: *The Popes, the Pill and the People* (Bruce).

Clemens, Alphonse H.: *Design for Successful Marriage* (Prentice-Hall).

Congar, Yves: *Lay People in the Church* (Newman Press).

Cronin, John F.: *Christianity and Social Progress. A Commentary on Mater et Magistra* (Helicon).

Cronin, John F.: *Social Principles and Economic Life* (Bruce).

D'Agostino, Angelo A. (ed.): *Family, Church, and Community* (Kenedy).

Danielou, Jean: *The Lord of History, Reflections on the Inner Meaning of History* (Regnery).

D'Arcy, Eric: *Conscience and Its Rights to Freedom* (Sheed and Ward).

D'Arcy, Martin: *The Meaning and Matter of History* (Farrar, Straus).

Dawson, Christopher H.: *Enquiries Into Religion and Culture* (Sheed and Ward).

Dawson, Christopher H.: *The Historic Reality of Christian Culture* (Harper).

Dawson, Christopher H.: *Religion and Culture* (Sheed and Ward).

Flannery, Harry W. (ed.): *Patterns for Peace: Catholic Statements on International Peace* (Newman Press).

Fremantle, Anne (ed.): *The Papal Encyclicals and Their Historical Context* (New American Library).

Gurian, Waldemar, and Fitzsimmons, Mark A. (ed).: *The Catholic Church in World Affairs* (U. of Notre Dame Press).

Hollis, Christopher: *Christianity and Economics* (Hawthorn).

Leclercq, Jacques: *The Christian and World Integration* (Hawthorn).

Leclercq, Jacques: *Marriage and the Family* (F. Pustet).

Lestapis, Stanislas de: *Family Planning and Modern Problems* (Herder and Herder).

Lubac, Henri de: *Catholicism: A Study of Dogma in Relation to the Corporate Destiny of Mankind* (Sheed and Ward).

Luzbetak, Louis J.: *The Church and Cultures: An Applied Anthropology for the Religious Worker* (Divine Word Publications, Techny, Ill.)

Lynch, William F.: *Christ and Apollo: The Dimensions of the Literary Imagination* (Sheed and Ward).

Mascall, E. L.: *Christian Theology and Natural Science, Some Questions on Their Relations* (Longmans).

Mascall, E. L.: *Theology and Images* (Mowbray).

Maritain, Jacques: *Man and the State* (U. of Chicago Press).

Masse, Benjamin L.: *Justice for All* (Bruce).

Melsen, Andreas G.: *Science and Technology* (Duquesne U. Press).

Messner, Johannes: *Social Ethics: Natural Law in the Modern World* (B. Herder).

Montini, Giovanni Battista: *The Church* (Helicon).

Moody, Joseph N. (ed.): *Church and Society* (Arts).

Moody, Joseph N., and Lawler, J. George (ed.): *The Challenge of Mater et Magistra* (Herder and Herder).

121

Murray, John Courtney: *The Problem of God, Yesterday and Today* (Yale U. Press).

Murray, John Courtney: *We Hold These Truths, Catholic Reflections on the American Proposition* (Sheed and Ward).

Murphy, Joseph S. (ed.): *Christianity and Culture* (Helicon).

Nagle, William J. (ed.): *Morality and Modern War* (Helicon).

Newman, Jeremiah: *The Christian in Society* (Helicon).

Noonan, John T.: *Contraception: A History of its Treatment by the Catholic Theologians and Canonists* (Harvard U. Press).

O'Gara, James (ed.): *The Layman in the Church* (Herder and Herder).

Planque, Daniel: *The Christian Couple* (Fides).

Regan, Richard J.: *American Pluralism and the Catholic Conscience* (Macmillan).

Riga, Peter: *Peace on Earth: A Commentary on Pope John's Encyclical* (Herder and Herder).

Rommen, Heinrich A.: *The Natural Law* (B. Herder).

Rommen, Heinrich A.: *The State in Catholic Thought* (B. Herder).

St. John-Stevas, Norman: *Birth Control and Public Policy* (Center for the Study of Democratic Institutions).

Sertillanges, Antonin G.: *The Intellectual Life, Its Spirit, Conditions, Methods* (Newman Press).

Simon, Yves R.: *Philosophy of Democratic Government* (U. of Chicago Press).

Sturzo, Luigi: *Church and State* (U. of Notre Dame Press).

Suenens, Leon Joseph Cardinal: *Love and Control: The Contemporary Problem* (Newman Press).

Tavard, George H.: *The Church Tomorrow* (Herder and Herder).

Teilhard de Chardin, Pierre: *The Divine Milieu* (Harper).

Thomas, John L.: *The Catholic Viewpoint on Marriage and the Family* (Hanover House).

Thompson, Charles S.: *Morals and Missiles* (J. Clarke).

Voillaume, Rene: *Seeds of the Desert* (Fides).

Weigel, Gustave: *The Modern God: Faith in a Secular Culture* (Macmillan).

Werth, Alvin (ed.): *Papal Pronouncements on Marriage and the Family From Leo XIII to Pius XII (1878-1954)* (Bruce).

Wicker, Brian: *Culture and Liturgy* (Sheed and Ward).

INDEX

Prepared by Joseph W. Sprug

Librarian, Loretto Heights College, Loretto, Colorado

124

creature unintelligible without
the creator, 34
fashioned anew, 2
man the center of, 12
subjection of all things to man,
32
(*see also* Nature)
Creatures:
proper use of, 34
Culture:
authors and artisans of, 57
autonomy, 58
benefits extended to all, 9
Christian spirit, 64
Christian unity, 58
Christianity and, 60
Church's missionary use of, 60
Church's promotion of, 61
classical; and modern technology, 58
conditions impeding, 63
conscious of right to, 63
development of the whole person, 58
duties of Christians, 62
dynamism and expansion of, 58
education to higher degree of, 28
elevation of mankind; learning
and arts, 59
harmony with Christian teaching, 64
help for those poor in, 60
heritage of tradition, 58
home education of children, 63
keep pace with science and technology, 65
legitimate autonomy, 62
liberty necessary for, 61
living exchange, 44
meaning for the person, 64
minorities, 62
modern characteristics, 57
new ways for extension of, 57
plurality of cultures, 56
as political or economic instrument, 62
possibility for full development,
63
profit for the Church, 44
proper development of, 56
renewal through Christianity, 61
respect and inviolability, 61
responsibility for progress of, 58
right of all men to, 62
safeguarding cultures, 58

sociological sense, 56
subordination to person and
community, 61
true and full humanity, 56
union with men of the time, 65
universal, 63
universal form of, 57
values in, 60
vocation of man, 59
the word, 56
Dead, The:
faith and, 16
Death:
anxiety over, 16
Christ's victory over, 16
example of Christ, 21
meaningful in Christ, 21
Democracy:
choice of systems and rulers, 79
Desire:
human longings, 35
imbalance in heart of man, 9
satisfaction of, 38
Despair:
modern problem, 12
riddles of life and death, 19
Developing nations. *see* Underdeveloped areas.
Devil:
struggle against powers of darkness, 34
Dictatorship:
violation of rights, 80
Dignity:
basis of, 16
Church and, 38
Church and the world, 37
concern for neighbor, 25
conscience and, 15
conjugal love, 53
culture and, 62
in economic and social life, 67
equality of persons, 27
false autonomy and, 39
ferment of the Gospel, 25
free choice, 15
God and human autonomy, 39
growing awareness of, 24
human body, 13, 39
husband and wife, 50
insults to human, 25
living conditions and, 28
love in marriage, 50
the married state, 48
modern man, 12

mutual respect for, 22
peace and, 85
politico-juridical order, 77
public and private institutions, 27
religion and, 19
the sick and the aged, 70
social betterment and the Church's message, 20
social order, 8
work for, 97
Disarmament:
beginning of, 89
Discrimination:
all forms rejected, 26
economic inequalities, 69
laboring classes; wages, 70
right to culture, 62
Discussion:
solutions to problems, 42
Divine law. *see* Law, Divine.
Divorce:
plague of, 47
profanation, 50

Earth:
development of, 59
divine plan for, 73
Economic assistance:
duty of advanced nations, 93
world commerce and developing nations, 92-93
Economic conditions:
balance lacking, 68
dignity of man, 67
extravagance and wretchedness together, 67
inequalities; discrimination, 69
international aspects, 68
reform needed, 68
Economic development:
determination by largest possible number of people, 69
false liberty, 69
growth, 69
international agencies, 93-94
international organization, 93
material and spiritual aspects, 94
mitigation of social inequalities, 67
mobility of workers, 70
progress depends on utilization of resources, 93
service of the whole man, 68

world commerce and developing nations, 92
Economic goods:
national wisdom and, 14
Economic problems:
aggressive demand for benefits, 8
untimely solutions, 94
Economics:
domination by, 67
international order, 93
modern characteristics, 67
the person superior in, 71
Education:
family life, 49
opportunities for, 63
provision for higher studies, 62
social aspects, 28
(*see also* Culture)
Education and state:
atheism, 18
Elections:
civil right and duty, 80
Employment:
creation of opportunities for, 70
End of the world:
time unknown, 36
Enemies:
love of, 26
Equality:
of all men, 26
Error. *see* Truth.
Eucharist:
foretaste of the heavenly banquet, 36
strength for life's journey, 35-36
Evangelization:
accommodated preaching, 44
civilization and, 106
Evil. *see* Good and evil.

Faith:
future life and, 16
as knowledge, 61
life penetrated by, 19
modern conditions, 7
new light on life, 11
Fall of man:
revelation and experience, 13
Family:
associations, 55
causes of discord, 8
Christ and, 29
communion of minds in, 53-54
community of love, 47
educational role, 63

foundation of society, 54
judgment of parents on number
of children, 95
large, 52
manifestation of Christ's presence, 49
material and spiritual conditions, 52
nobility of, 47
promotion of values of, 54-55
social changes and, 47

Farmers:
culture and, 63
income, 70
modern conditions, 9

Fathers:
family life, 54

Fidelity:
in marriage, 48

Finance:
international, 74
international cooperation, 92

Freedom:
atheism and, 18
crippled by poverty, 28
human activity joined with religion, 33
of inquiry, thought and expression, 66
license and, 15
private ownership, 74
strength; social aspects, 28

Friendship:
in marriage, 50

Future:
dominion over, 5

Future life:
earthly values perfected in, 36
faith in, 16
human longings, 36

God:
autonomy of man and, 39
Church as witness to, 19
human longings for, 38

Good and evil:
duty to fight evil, 21
experience of the Fall of man, 13
freedom necessary for goodness, 15
indifference to goodness, 26
questions remain, despite progress, 10
social circumstances as factor in, 23-24

struggle against powers of darkness, 34

Grace:
acknowledgment of the Word, 59
works unseen, 21

Guilt:
judgments about internal, 26

Happiness:
progress and, 34

History:
advances in, 57
becoming all of a piece, 6
Christ and, 35
Christ the center of, 45
Christ the key to, 10
Church has profited by, 44
Church's role in, 38
consummation of, 45
private, disappearing, 6

Holy Spirit:
Christ in the heart of man, 35
Christians led by, 1
Church and, 19
diverse gifts of, 35
fidelity of the Church, 43
gift: knowledge of the divine plan, 15
impulses of, 99
man renewed by, 21
resurrection of man, 21
social order and, 25
unity of the Church, 40

Hope:
resurrection, 21
temporal and eternal, 19

Human activity. see Activity.

Human body. see Body, Human.

Human race. see Man.

Human relations:
respect and love for those of differing views, 26
sports and, 64
union of the faithful with men of the times, 65

Humanism:
autonomy of culture and, 58
denial of God or religion, 7
emancipation and rule by human efforts, 10
new; extension of responsibility, 58

Hunger:
sharing earthly goods, 73

political life, 78
principles worked out by the Church, 68
social order, 24-25

Kingdom of God:
earthly progress and, 36
mission of the Church, 45
present on earth in mystery, 36
Knowledge:
certitude about reality, 14
faith and reason: two orders, 61

Labor and laboring classes:
culture and, 63
disgraceful conditions, 25
disputes and negotiations, 72
leisure, 71
mobility, 70
modern conditions, 9
organization adapted to persons, 71
persons, not tools of production, 70
provision for technical and professional formation, 70
superiority of the person, 70-71
workers as slaves, 71
workers share in determining conditions, 72
Labor unions:
responsibility in economic development, 72
right to form, 72
Laity:
formation in sacred sciences, 66
freedom of inquiry, thought and expression, 66
secular duties and activities, 41
teaching authority of the Church, 42
witnesses to Christ, 42
Land:
distribution of ownership, 94
reforms of ownership for the common good, 75
Law:
observance of just laws, 27
Law, Divine:
human rights and, 39
laity and establishment of, 42
Lazarus:
concern for, 25
Learning and scholarship:
blend new sciences with Chris-

tian teaching, 65
Christian faith and, 64
elevation of mankind, 59
method; religious aspects, 33
pastoral care and secular sciences, 64
synthesis, 58
synthesis difficult to form, 63
Leisure:
increase of, 63-64
laboring classes, 71
modern culture, 57
Liberty:
authority compatible with, 81
culture, development of, 61
temporary restriction of rights, 80
Life:
eternal destiny of man, 53
safeguarding, 53
things opposed to, 25
Literature:
in life of the Church, 64
Liturgy:
art and, 65
culture and, 60-61
Love:
Church manifests God's love for men, 45
common good, 27
conscience and, 15
of created things, 34
of enemies, 26
first and greatest commandment, 22
God's presence revealed by, 19
human: affection of the will, 50
human recognition of divine, 17
in marriage, 55
in ordinary circumstances of life, 35
peace and, 85
social order, 24-25
for those who think or act differently, 26
truth and, 99
truth and error; indifference, 26
war vanquished by, 86
world problems and, 98
world's transformation, 35
(see also Marriage; Sex)

Man:
activity, 32
basic questions of modern man, 10

131

biblical teaching, 12
bodily composition, 13
center of all things on earth, 12
Christ the key to mystery of, 10
creature as rival of Creator, 32
desire for a higher life, 16
desires and limitations, 9
destiny, 14
develop the earth, 59
development of human faculties, 61
development; social aspects, 23
dignity of, *see* Dignity.
dynamic, evolutionary concept of reality, 6
emancipated by Christ, 2
exaltation and despair, 12
find self through gift of self, 23
grandeur and misery, 13
guiding forces unleashed by, 9
humanity an offering accepted by God, 35
image of universal man, 63
imbalance in heart of, 9
interior qualities, 14
isolation, 29
literature and arts, 64
male and female, 12
mandate over nature, 31-32
material and spiritual needs, 68-69
meaning of his existence, 38
modern anxiety, 2
modern new stage of history, 4
mutual service in answering questions of, 11
mystery of, and the Incarnation, 20
new creature in the Holy Spirit, 34
political formation, 79
preserved by God's love, 16-17
puzzle to himself, 19
reality in heart of, 14
restoration of divine likeness, 20
reverence for, 25
sanctified by Christ, 39
service of men, 59
social nature of, 12
struggle with good and evil, 13
as sufficient to himself, 60
superior to bodily concerns, 13-14
unity of, 13

value in what he is, 32
the whole man, 2
wisdom, 14
(*see also* Humanism; Person; Society; *etc.*)
Marriage:
childless, 52
Christ and the Church as model, 48
conjugal love; divine law, 52
cooperation with love of the Creator, 51
danger when intimacy broken off, 53
dignity and value, 48
disfigurements of, 47
faithfulness and harmony in, 51
fidelity in, 48
friendship, 50
God the author of, 48
husband and wife: true love, 50
irrevocable covenant, 48
love in, 49
mutual help and service, 48
mutual love, growth of, 52
nobility of, 47
pastoral counseling, 55
perfection in, 48
power and strength of the institution, 47
preparation for, 54
procreation and education of children, 48, 51
profaned by self-love, 47
promotion of values of, 54-55
pure love; undivided affection, 50
renewal in, 51
responsible parenthood, 52
sacrament; consecration, 49
sex in, 50
virtue demanded in, 50
vocation; witness to Christ, 55
Martyrs:
witness to faith, 19
Materialism:
culture and, 59
problem for modern man, 10
Migrants:
international agencies, 92
Migration:
social shanges, 6
Military service:
proper role of, 87

132

Minorities:
  culture; liberty, 62
  political rights, 77
Modern world. *see* Civilization,
  Modern.
Moral education:
  parents' responsibility, 95
Moral order:
  economic aspects, 69
  political authority, 79
Morality:
  individualistic, 27
  keep pace with science and tech-
    nology, 65
  objective norms of, 15
Mothers:
  domestic role, 54

Nations, Developing. *see* Underdeveloped areas.
Natural law:
  permanent binding force, 86
Nature:
  control over, 8
  culture and, 56
  mastery over, 31
  sanctified by Christ, 39
Necessities:
  available to all men, 24
Neighbor:
  as another self, 25
  every man, 25

Obedience:
  civil obligation, 79
Old age:
  dignity; livelihood, 70
  parents and children, 49
Order:
  peace, 85

Parents:
  community of love, 47
  education and welfare of chil-
    dren, 95
  judgment of family size, 52
  mission: transmission of life, 51
  old age; children, 49
  religious example of, 49
  (*see also* Children; Family)
Passion:
  dignity and, 15
Past:
  dominion over, 5

Pastoral work:
  secular sciences and, 64
  vocation of married people, 55
Pastors:
  daily conduct and concern, 43
  laity and, 42
Patriotism:
  cultivation of, 81
Peace:
  arms as deterrents to war, 88
  causes of, 84-85
  ceaseless efforts for, 85
  Christian unity and, 99
  community of nations, 84
  contribution of the Church to, 96
  cooperation in achieving, 84
  economic inequality and, 68
  enterprise of justice, 84
  eternal life, 36
  false hope, 91
  instruction in sentiments of, 90
  international bodies working for,
    91
  join with all true peacemakers,
    85
  love of neighbor, 85
  military service and, 87
  mutual trust essential, 89
  personal aspects, 85
  studies of the problem, 90
  working together for, 99
Perfection:
  common good, 78
  culture and, 61
  love and, 35
  in marriage, 48-49
Persecution:
  Justin and Tertullian on, 104
  profit from, 45
Person:
  culture and perfection of, 61
  laboring classes, 71
  preservation of, 2
  social order to benefit the, 24
  socialization, 80
  transcendent character; Church
    as sign, 82
  understanding the whole, 63
  violations of integrity of, 25
Personality:
  modern development, 38
  private property and, 74
Philosophy:
  Church's use of, 44

133

Reason:
    faith and, 61
Refugees:
    international agencies, 92
Relief work:
    Catholic organism proposed, 97
    duty of, 73
    international volunteers, 96
Religion:
    earthly affairs and, 41
    indifference to problems of, 38
    modern conditions affecting, 7
Religions:
    Catholic Church's esteem for, 38
    recognition of diversity, 98
    respect for, 77
Religious education:
    family life, 49
Religious practice:
    modern abandonment of, 7
Responsibility:
    family size, 95
    increasing sense of, 57-58
    new humanism, 58
    relative to power, 32
    sense of, 28
    universal, 97
Resurrection of the body:
    Christian hope, 21
    future blessedness, 36
Revelation:
    culture and, 60
Rights:
    cooperation to guarantee for all
        people, 77
    cultural autonomy and, 61
    discrimination rejected, 26
    divine law and, 39
    dynamic movements of modern
        world, 39
    false autonomy, 39
    government recognition of, 41
    growing discovery of, 38
    protection of, 77
    restricted for the common good,
        80
    system for protection of, 80
    universal and inviolable, 24
Rulers, Civil:
    protection of rights, 80

Sabbath:
    made for man, 24
Sacred sciences:
    study by the laity, 66

Salvation:
    mission of the Church, 45
    news of, 1
    temporal duties and, 41
Sanctification:
    in marriage, 49
Scholarship. see Learning and
    scholarship.
Science:
    agnosticism and, 60
    autonomy of, 62
    denial of God or religion, 7
    keeping pace with, 65
    meaning for the person, 64
    modern culture, 57
    modern intellectual formation, 5
    values in, 60
Science and religion:
    method; no conflict, 33
    new findings and faith, 64
Scientific method:
    limitations of, 60
Self:
    gift of self, 23
Selfishness:
    social disturbance, 24
Self-knowledge:
    advances in, 6
Sex:
    dignity in conjugal love, 53
    in marriage, 50
    true practice of conjugal love, 51
Sin:
    allurements of, 61
    bondage, 39
    certitude obscured by, 14
    conscience and habitual sin, 15
    earthly and heavenly city, 37-38
    fulfillment of man blocked by,
        13
    inducements to, 24
    rebellious stirrings in the body,
        13
Slavery:
    fight against, 27
    social and psychological, 5
Social action:
    Christians fighting for justice, 75
    rights to culture, 62
Social change:
    in institutions, 77
    intellectual and technological
        aspects, 5
    modern cultural and social
        transformation, 4

135

political aspects, 77
questioning accepted values, 7
in traditional local communities,
  6
Social conditions:
  culture impeded by, 63
  dignity of man, 67
  excessive economic and social
    differences, 27
  a more unified world, 28
  work for betterment of, 19-20
Social ethics:
  cultural and educational obliga-
    tions, 28
  observance of obligations, 28
  observe social necessities, 28
Social groups:
  interrelationship, 24
Social institutions:
  dealing with destination of
    earthly goods, 73
  subject and goal of, 23
Social justice:
  Catholic organism proposed, 97
Social order:
  Church's activities in behalf of,
    40
  constant improvement, 24
  destruction of the human race,
    34
  disturbances, 24
  founded on truth, justice, love,
    24-25
  service and dignity of man, 8
  work for benefit of the person,
    24
Social problems:
  assistance for every man, 97
  conditions poisoning society, 25
  marriage and family problems,
    48
  special urgency, 46
Social reform:
  necessity of, 68
Social relations:
  participation in, 28
Social sciences:
  advances in, 6
Socialization:
  advantages to the person, 23
  effects, 6
  human autonomy and, 80
  worthy elements in, 40
Society:
  basic truths about, 22

Church as leaven of, 37
culture and, 61
moral and spiritual nature of
  man, 22
renewal, 2
uncertainty of direction, 4
Sociology:
  pastoral use, 64
Solidarity:
  authority and freedom, 81
  Church and the world, 2
  Eucharist and, 36
  international cooperation, 92
  mutual dependence, 5
  perfection; future life, 30
  scientific studies and, 60
  social unity, 29
  universal, 97
Soul:
  recognition of, 14
Spirit:
  human culture, 59
Spirituality:
  national traditions, 94
Sports:
  value of, 64
State, The:
  economic policy, 67
  intervention in social, economic
    and cultural matters, 80
  (see also Politics)
Strikes:
  recourse to, 72
Study:
  leisure and, 64
Subsidiarity:
  international community, 93
Suffering:
  example of Christ, 21
Superstition:
  modern view of religion, 7
Talents:
  service of God and man, 39
Taxes:
  avoiding, 27
Technology:
  agnosticism and, 60
Technology and civilization:
  classical culture and, 58
  keeping pace with science, 65
  mounting importance of, 5
  transforming the earth, 5
Temporal goods:
  common, in extreme necessity,
    107

136

customs related to modern needs, 73

duty to be concerned with this world, 36

earthly vocation, 35

neglect of, 41

New Testament teaching on use, 108

political and economic progress, 8-9

right to sufficient share, 73

science, learning and religion, 33

share in, 73

superfluous, 107

use in Church's mission, 82

Temporal order:
apostolate, 82
Christian service to, 99
man's eternal vocation, 82
mission of the Church, 83

Theology:
communicating to men of the times, 64
studies in contact with the times, 65
teachers collaborate with men of science, 65

Time:
dominion over, 5

Totalitarianism:
violation of rights, 80

Tourism:
value of, 64

Trade unions. see Labor unions.

Trinity:
unity, 23

Truth:
conscience and search for, 15
free search for, 62
love and, 99
love and indifference to error, 26
scientific method and, 60
social order, 24-25

Underdeveloped areas:
dependence increasing, 9
development requires changes in world commerce, 92
industrialization and urbanization, 7
investments in, 74
landowners and tenants, 75
progress a duty in, 69
volunteer services in, 96

(*see also* Economic development)

Unity:
Christian unity and, 99
human family founded on Christ, 40
mankind and the Trinity, 23
mission of the Church, 98
preservation of civilizations, 57
promotion of, 40
(*see also* Solidarity)

Unity of the Church:
social unity and, 40

Universal community. see Internationalism.

Universe:
intellect and, 14

Values:
change in attitudes, 7
cultural, 58
development of culture, 56-57
disordered, 34
the human person, 63
man, 32
modern civilization, 5
modern culture, 60
purification of, 11
science and civilization, 60
temporal and eternal, 36
universal, 59

Violence:
renunciation of use of, 85-86
vanquishing of, 85-86

Virtues:
moral and social, 28

Vocation:
earthly duties of Christians, 41
earthly service, 35
human activity, 33

Voting:
civil right, 79-80

Wages:
discrimination in, 70
sufficiency, 71

War:
arms race as cause, 89
attitudes towards, 90
avoidance of, 86
causes, 91
criminal actions, 86
danger increasing, 89
destruction of entire cities, 88
freedom from slavery of, 89

guerrilla warfare, 86
hazard of modern weapons, 88
international agreements, 86
leaders working to eliminate, 90
massive and indiscriminate destruction, 87
outlawed by international consent, 89
right to legitimate defense, 87
seeking conquest of other nations, 87
terrorism, 86
threat of, 84
threat vanquished by love, 86
total slaughter, 87
weapons as deterrents, 88
weapons of modern science, 86
Wealth:
modern conditions, 4
passionate desires for, 75
squandering, 67
Wealth, Distribution of:
dependence of developing nations, 9
unequal, 95-96
Weapons. *see* War.
Widowhood:
continuation of the marriage vocation, 49
Wisdom:
attraction of, 14
eternal, 59
nations rich in, 14
observation and, 58

Woman:
cultural life, 63
domestic role, 54
equality in law and in fact, 9
rights not universally honored, 26-27
Work:
development of self, 32
duty and right, 71
results of, 71
subjection of all things; divine plan, 32
Working classes. *see* Labor and laboring classes.
World:
biblical usage of the word, 34
presence and activity of the Church in, 2
(*see also* Temporal order)
World community:
growing recognition of, 31
(*see also* International organization)
Worship:
spirit drawn to, 59

Youth:
culture, 63
international community and, 97
political formation, 81
preparation for marriage, 51
questioning of accepted values, 7